Hoyle T. Allred is a B.A. graduate of Guilford College, Greensboro, N.C., and holds the M.Div. and D.Min. Degrees from Southern Baptist Theological Seminary, Louisville, Kentucky. He was a pastor in North Carolina for eighteen years before coming to his present position as Director of Missions of the Gaston Baptist Association.

Dr. Allred began his Associational work as a layman prior to World War II, working in the Training Union organization of the Piedmont Baptist Association of North Carolina. During Seminary days he served in several capacities with the White's Run Baptist Association of Kentucky, and upon graduation returned to Greensboro, North Carolina where he worked with veteran Missionary T.L. Sasser as Associational Clerk. He also served the Stanley Baptist Association of North Carolina in several capacities, including Moderator.

In the Baptist State Convention the author has served on several committees and chaired the Committee on Committees and Public Affairs Committee, and also served as chairman of the General Board's Evangelism Committee for two years. In addition, he has worked in State summer assemblies and led conferences for the Home Mission Board at Glorieta and Ridgecrest.

Without

Trumpets

Hoyle T. Allred

MOORE PUBLISHING COMPANY
Durham, North Carolina 27705

Library of Congress Catalog Card Number: 76-57851

ISBN 0-87716-079-1

CONTENTS

Without Trumpets

PREFACE

My interest was first kindled in missions when I was less than five years old and was called on to sing a song in Sunday School. With a child's limited vocabulary, I had misunderstood the words of a song and remember the gales of laughter from teachers and others when I sang:

Right in the corner where you are,
Right in the corner where you are,
Someone far from harbor you may
guide across the bar,
Right in the corner where you are.

Although they laughed, I have found in later years, that my childish misunderstanding of the message is contemporary missions!

When I grew beyond the naivete of childhood and learned that the money from the offering plates was not taken to heaven by the golden rays of the sun shining through storm clouds, but that God used the money as Christians shared it in meeting the needs of mankind in this world with the gospel of Jesus, doubts were shown in my mind about giving to missions by the arguments of older men who believed that the church could make better use of its money than sending it to some new and nebulous Cooperative Program of missions. I asked my pastor, J. Ben

Eller, if the men were right and if maybe the local church ought to keep the money at home and use it in that low-income to middle class neighborhood, where there were many unmet needs. The pastor's reply was indelible, as he placed his hand on my shoulders: "Most of it will be used in this church community to meet its needs for the gospel of Jesus, but we must always keep our eyes on the far corners of the world and all the area in between, knowing it, too, has need for the same message being preached." He explained to me that if the church were faithful in sharing, then it was up to those who received the gifts to be faithful. He explained, "It is required of a steward to be faithful." "Their responsibility is not yours," he said. "God will judge them."

Later, in working with Vacation Bible Schools, I claimed this moto: "I will do the best I can, with what I have, where I am for Jesus' sake today." I pray all others will do the same.

A God-given encounter led me to know that the local church was not doing enough to share the gospel with the rest of the world. The realization came when a Jewish man became "completed" in Jesus Christ and asked me, through tearful eyes one Sunday morning, "When are your people going to stop preaching to themselves and do something to bring my people to Christ?" It was then that I took a closer look at what was being done in the local church and found that too much was being done to preach the gospel to ourselves and not nearly enough to preach to the rest of the world.

My ministry took a decided change and I tried to lead the church out of the walls of its building to tell others about Jesus. I have never concerned myself to a great extent that someone might abuse that which was entrusted to them, because of my pastor's words of years before to be found faithful, and leave the rest to God. With the help of God I still try to work right in the corner where I am, believing that God can accomplish more than I can when I am found faithful. Others have the awesome responsibility of accounting to God for their corners of service. I am willing to let them stand on their stewardship and I on mine.

The book is being named *Without Trumpets* because people beyond the geographical bounds of Gaston County, and even many within, are not aware of the strong cooperative support of missons given by Gaston Baptists. This is evidenced by the fact that pastors and laymen of the Association are seldom named to the Boards, Agencies and Committees of North Carolina Baptists, although their record is far stronger than that of adjoining associations, but they are passed over and selections made from nearby cities of Charlotte and Shelby. It is also the hope of this writer that a trumpet *will* sound within the Association to cause us to give no less *percentage-wise*, that is at least *20%, undesignated*, to the Cooperative Program, than was given in the early days of the Association.

This present writing is a re-writing of my doctoral thesis entitled *A Strategy for Increasing Gifts to Cooperative Missions from Member Churches of the Gaston Baptist Association, (N. C.)*. Permission to do so was granted by the Progessional Studies Committee of the Southern Baptist Theological Seminary, and appreciation is here expressed not only for this permission but for their aid in completing the original work.

I feel that whatever is good about this writing is the

result of the efforts of countless people who have taught and trained me across the years. My appreciation is expressed especially to the pastors and laymen of the Gaston Baptist Association for so ably assisting in gathering material and providing data. Without them this record could not have been written.

My family has borne more than their share of family responsibilities and provided emotional warmth, strength, and encouragement during the busy months. I am deeply grateful. Next summer we'll plow up the back yard and plant a garden!

Appreciation is expressed to these and all others with the desire that this writing be used as a part of our total stewardship before God for His glory.

The team effort is now bread cast upon the waters.

HOYLE T. ALLRED

Gastonia, N. C.
Summer 1975

A CLEAR LOOK AT WHAT IT IS ABOUT

The "Ridgecrest Statement" on Associational Missions, following the May 1974 National Convocation on the Southern Baptist Association; pointed up ten points of major concern for the Baptist Association. Point three of the statement pointed out the following:[1]

1. The role of the Association should be identified by its major concerns (purpose or objectives).
2. It is the unit geographically closest to the churches of the Association.
3. It is urged to recognize (understand) its setting and to assist the churches in their mission.
4. The Association is encouraged to self study to determine its nature, needs, objectives, resources and opportunities.
5. It is encouraged to share its findings to strengthen state and Southern Baptist Convention agencies.

As the Director of Missions of the Gaston Association (N. C.), I was encouraged by Associational leadership to study at the Southern Baptist Theological Seminary in 1973-74 in the area of Associational Administration. In reading the Ridgecrest Statement, I found that the first four points of the Ridgecrest Statement were the subject of my doctrinal thesis. To share my findings (Point five above) is the purpose of this re-writing.

I believe that this study will be a guide to other Associations or Directors of Associational Missions in coming to know how to go about understanding their own settings that they might determine their nature, needs, objectives, resources and opportunities in a similar fashion. The Gaston Association (N. C.) is the best area of the Old South to use as a model to study because of its history, geographical location (at the center of the South's textile industry) and its odious connection with the so-called Loray Mill labor dispute of 1929.[2]

The Gaston Association would be typical of many in the Old South where the churches are peopled largely with the working class. The writing will show how the Association, shaped by its geography and social setting, has faced up to its responsibility for helping churches to fulfil their mission in their setting.

This Association, from its beginning has been a leader in Cooperative Mission gifts to State and Southern Baptist Convention agencies and institutions, but the study revealed where its's pride was the greatest it had fallen the lowest in accomplishing its stated purposes and objectives when compared to itself. It then seeks to understand the causes and to project a strategy to overcome the deficiencies.

The tools of Social Research are used and must needs be the tools for any Association or Director of Missions in coming to grips with their tasks in creating that which Russell Bennett calls "a fellowship through which the churches, in the spirit of Christ, serve one another."[3]

THE GASTON BAPTIST ASSOCIATION

I. Setting

Historical. In time for Christmas, 1846, the legislature of the State of North Carolina created the State's seventy-fourth county. It was carved from Lincoln County and named Gaston for Judge William Gaston, statesman, scholar, benefactor and State Supreme Court Justice who had died in January of 1844.[1]

The county, four hundred square miles in land area, was populated by some 8,000 inhabitants including a remnant of the once great tribe of the Catawba Indians and a twenty-five percent population of Negro slaves.

Whites had been in the area since the late 17th Century. They came as traders down the famed Virginia Trading Path from the James River in Virginia and up the riverside paths from Charleston in South Carolina. Settlement began at Tuckaseegee Ford on land "generously" provided by the Catawbas. Their generosity was repaid with an epidemic of smallpox which reduced the tribe to a scattered few Indians to be found west of the South Fork.

Early white settlers chose the area between the South Fork and the Catawba Rivers to establish their holdings. This well-watered area would produce verdant farms at first and later provide water power for the first textile mills to be established in Gaston County. These landed settlers of

Scotch-Irish and German descent brought their Lutheran and Presbyterian faiths with them and soon established churches called Goshen and Kastner's (now Philadelphia). Meanwhile the almost penniless settlers claimed and cleared land west of the South Fork and began worship beneath a white grape arbor near a large rock. Adjacent to the area they began to bury their dead and hallow the spot as Brush Arbor Church.[2] This church was reorganized into the Long Creek Baptist Church in 1772. A log structure was built to serve as a church and school for Baptist children who, until this time, had not been permitted to attend the school held in Kastner's Church.[3]

The legislature of 1846 included in its enactment establishing Gaston County:

... Be it further enacted, that ... are hereby appointed commissioners to select and determine upon a site for a permanent seat of justice for said county, who shall locate the same as near the centre as a suitable location can be obtained, provided it shall be within two miles of Long Creek Baptist Church meeting house.[4]

Long Creek was a charter church in the organization of the Gaston Baptist Association in 1919. Therefore, Gaston Baptists have roots in the historical origins of Gaston County and have survived the years to become the county's most numerous and influential church group.

Geographical. Gaston County is strategically located in about the geographical center of the Piedmont Plateau. It lies equidistant between Danville, Virginia, and Anderson, South Carolina, the north and south boundaries generally considered by geologists as the Piedmont Plateau. An abundant water supply which begins at the eastern continental divide near Ridgecrest, North Carolina, flows through tributaries to form the Catawba waterway. In origin the waterway provided hydro power for early industries. The Duke interests established a system of water control and now electrical power is provided by the Catawba for much of the region. This ready source of power, amidst abundant cotton fields and its central location and proximity to unskilled labor in the mountains nearby, attracted early industry to Gaston County. These factors continue to be important to the prosperity of the region.

Early major East-West and North-South highways transversed the county giving it access to the markets of the world. The laying of the Southern Railway through North Carolina connecting New Orleans with New York brought a change in the county seat.

Dallas, the county seat since 1846, did not want the railroad. Gastonia aided the company. The right-of-way divided Gastonia into North and South sectors. This division created problems which still remain; however, not enough division to prevent a successful county vote in 1911 to move the county seat to Gastonia.

Gaston County is characterized by numerous small mountains and secondary streams. Early roads ran by the rivers and streams around the base of the mountains. Towns sprang up anywhere roads met and streams flowed together providing power sufficient to run a mill. This peculiarity of the region created thirteen moderate sized incorporated towns[5] with their attendant jealousies and rivalries. These factors continue to influence local politics

TABLE I

GASTON COUNTY POPULATION BY TOWNS AND TOWNSHIPS

1910 - 1990

Town or Township	1910	1920	1930	1940	1950	1960	1970	1980	1990
Cherryville Twp.	4,328	5,390	7,179	7,529	8,907	9,171	9,648	10,062	9,863
Cherryville Town	1,153	1,884	2,756	3,225	3,492	3,607	4,104	4,276	4,187
Crowders Mtn. Twp.	4,382	3,859	6,218	6,149	7,145	7,461	7,200	7,546	7,178
Bessemer City Town	1,529	2,176	3,739	3,567	3,961	4,017	3,672	3,370	2,736
Dallas Twp.	4,384	4,566	5,667	6,181	8,969	10,357	12,528	15,428	18,112
Dallas Town	1,065	1,397	1,489	1,704	2,454	3,270	3,888	4,897	5,844
Gastonia Twp.	12,268	21,502	33,123	39,062	49,281	58,117	67,248	79,658	90,092
Gastonia City	5,759	12,871	17,093	21,313	23,069	37,276	49,599	61,576	70,346
River Bend Twp.	4,531	5,338	8,139	8,041	9,974	12,499	14,400	17,273	19,727
Mt. Holly Town	526	1,160	2,254	2,055	2,241	4,037	4,622	5,735	6,755
Stanley Town	321	584	1,084	1,036	1,644	1,913	2,347	2,918	3,443
South Point Twp.	7,170	10,587	17,772	20,569	26,560	29,469	32,976	37,733	41,128
Belmont City	1,176	2,941	4,121	4,356	5,330	5,007	5,342	5,534	5,378
Lowell Town	876	1,151	1,664	1,826	2,313	2,776	3,269	3,840	4,300
McAdenville Town	983	1,162	914	887	1,060	748	576	503	465
Totals	37,063	51,242	78,093	87,531	110,836	127,074	144,000	167,700	186,100

From: Population and Economy, p. 22.

in all social structures including the Gaston Baptist Association.

In 1973 Gastonia and Charlotte were merged for statistical reports by the United States Bureau of the Budget to form the Charlotte-Gastonia Standard Metropolitan Statistical Area. Predictions are that this strategically located area is to be at the heart of the nation's fifth largest urban area by 2000.[6]

Economic. Early Gaston County never knew the agricultural prosperity of the down east counties. Normally farms were small and self-sufficient but the "sell" crops were relatively low. Mines in the county yielded varying quantities of gold, lime, sulphur, tin and iron. Furnaces for smelting ore were founded early around Mount Holly, Bessemer City and High Shoals. One hardy early settler built an iron works which supplied the area with tools of iron.[7]

Between 1845 and 1848, an industrial boom hit the county. During this period three cotton mills were built and began operating at Mountain Island, Tuckaseegee (Mount Holly) and McAdenville. These mills and others, drawn by ready water power and other factors discussed above, were to dominate Gaston County's economic and industrial structure until the 1950's.[8]

Liston Pope said of the economic setting:

The economic culture of the community was organized in the general form loosely called capitalism. Further, it was capitalism at its peak of control over culture: capitalism extended through paternalism. The capitalist did not merely provide capital; he also established the facilities and set the

TABLE II

GASTON COUNTY EMPLOYMENT

1950 - 1990, Number and Percent of Total

	1950 No.	%	1960 No.	%	1970 No.	%	1980 No.	%	1990 No.	%
MANUFACTURING										
Machinery	819	1.79	3,259	6.37	4,608	8.0	6,375	9.5	8,184	11.0
Food and Kindred Prod.	314	.69	583	1.14	806	1.4	1,141	1.7	1,488	2.0
Textile & Apparel	24,353	53.22	21,509	42.05	21,888	38.0	22,948	34.2	22,469	30.2
Other Manufacturing	1,318	2.88	2,251	4.40	3,226	5.6	4,563	6.8	5,952	8.0
Total Manufacturing	26,804	58.58	27,602	53.96	30,528	53.0	35,027	52.2	38,093	51.2
NON-MANUFACTURING										
Agriculture	2,070	4.52	828	1.62	691	1.2	604	.9	446	.6
Construction	2,068	4.52	2,327	4.54	2,534	4.4	2,818	4.2	2,976	4.0
Transportation, Communication & Utilities	1,868	4.08	3,052	5.97	3,860	6.7	4,898	7.3	5,952	8.0
Trade	5,612	12.26	6,454	12.62	7,315	12.7	8,589	12.8	9,672	13.0
Service	4,759	10.40	4,991	9.77	5,300	9.2	5,771	8.6	5,952	8.0
Government	2,241	4.90	3,081	6.02	3,686	6.4	4,563	6.8	5,357	7.2
Other Non-manufacturing	337	.74	2,816	5.50	3,686	6.4	4,830	7.2	5,952	8.0
Total Non-manufacturing	18,955	41.42	23,549	46.04	27,072	47.0	32,073	47.8	36,307	48.8
TOTAL EMPLOYMENT	45,759	100.00	51,151	100.0	57,600	100.0	67,100	100.0	74,400	100.0

From: _Population and Economy_, p. 67

norms for politics, morals, religion, amusement, and all other major spheres of culture. His control and his moral right to control had hardly been questioned. Regulation of his activities had been minimal. In short, Gastonia was a stronghold, relatively isolated and undisturbed, of paternalistic capitalism.[9]

Then the Communists came to town (the presence and influence of communism being the most undisputed fact of the Loray Mill strike), and thrust this small industrial community onto the world stage with its open confrontation with paternalistic capitalism. According to the famed Loray strike leader, Fred E. Beal, it was Gaston County's geographic location in the center of the textile Piedmont and the relative isolationism of communities which led it to be chosen as the spot to organize the South.[10]

The Loray debacle (called "war" by locals involved) was a disaster but led the Gaston community to reassess its values and begin a long change toward diversified industry and non-manufacturing employment.

A comparison of Tables II and III will show, although industry became diversified, that in 1966 the two major employers of the county ranked eleventh and fifteenth in average wage paid.

10

TABLE III
N. C. EMPLOYMENT 1966

Industry Group	Rank by No. Employed	Rank by Avg. Earnings
Textiles	1	11
Apparel	2	15
Furniture	3	12
Food	4	13
Electric Machinery	5	8
Lumber	6	14
Tobacco	7	6
Other Machinery	8	9
Chemicals	9	4
Paper	10	1
Stone, Clay, Glass	11	10
Metals (Fabricated)	12	7
Printing	13	2
Ordinance & Trans. Equip.	14	5
Metals (Primary)	15	3

A study made in 1969 summed up the economic setting:

. . . The primary need for improving employment in Gaston is not simply acquiring new job opportunities but rather in acquiring jobs which rank high in earning ability for the worker. This will tend to improve the entire economic base of the county and place it in a better position to compete with nearby metropolitan Mecklenburg.

Basically Gaston is in the midst of a strong

employment period as jobs are increasing and unemployment is decreasing. The county has now reached the place, however, where it must consider quality of employment as well as quantity. Here rests the future economic well-being of the county.[11]

The change to home ownership and ending of child labor were other economic benefits to follow the Loray strike. Employees have come to home ownership of the small homes once provided by the mill companies as a part of compensation. These real estate holdings have created community pride and a stabilization of people and the economy.[12] Because of its stable economy, Gaston County's population growth has been rapid but consistent. The following tables speak for themselves:

TABLE IV

POPULATION ANALYSIS

SCHEDULE I - POPULATION GROWTH

Year	Gaston County	Gastonia
1890	17,764	1,033
1900	27,903	4,610
1910	37,063	5,759
1920	51,242	12,871
1930	78,093	17,093
1940	87,559	21,311
1950	110,836	23,389
1955-special enumeration		34,389
1960	127,074	37,276
1965	135,775	45,429
1970	148,415	47,613

SCHEDULE II - RACE ANALYSIS - 1970 Census

	Gaston County	%	Gastonia	%
White	130,165	87.7	39,486	83
Negro	18,020	12.3	8,105	17
Other Races	230		22	-
	148,415	100	47,613	100

SCHEDULE III - AGE ANALYSIS BY RACE - 1970 Census

	Gaston County				Gastonia			
	White	%	Non-White	%	White	%	Non-White	%
Under 24	59,704	46	9,792	54	17,071	44	4,200	52
25-44	33,593	26	3,631	20	9,874	25	1,688	21
45-64	27,242	21	3,327	19	8,798	22	1,626	20
Over 65	9,856	7	1,270	7	3,294	9	591	7
All Ages	130,395	100	18,020	100	39,037	100	8,105	100

SCHEDULE IV - POPULATION PER HOUSEHOLD - 1970 Census

Gaston County		Gastonia	
White	Non-White	White	Non-White
3.25	3.84	3.14	3.54

Child labor, an integral part of the economic plight of the poor South following the Civil War, was a necessity in those years as families moved from ruined farms where children had helped to produce meager income to the cities. The children were still needed to supply family necessities. However, like most institutions established out of necessity, child labor outlived its day and continued until abolished by law and the establishment of compulsory education in the late 1920's.

With diversification of employment and bettered education, Gaston County should rise in per capita income and family income[13] to rank better among the state's counties in the years ahead.

Social. Prior to World War II, Gaston County was a class society.[14] Following it, however, the barriers began to break down. The liberated G. I. used the G. I. Bill to return to school and acquire learning, trades, skills, and enter the professions. Children of mill workers became the community's doctors, lawyers, teachers, ministers, accountants, owners of small businesses and supervisory personnel in the mill management.

Many of them continued to live in or near the now occupant-owned mill villages. They mingled with other professionals and attracted them to the once mill church. These churches have problems which are occasioned by longevity of the founders, the influx of new people and educated children and grandchildren. The public distinction of uptown and mill churches no longer exists. Owners and professionals sit on church committees with employees and unemployed.

Each village once had its school to educate through the eighth grade. Most students completed this grade and then dropped out and entered the labor market. As late as 1962, to my knowledge, the drop-out rate was 50% by the ninth grade! The county and city systems merged and began construction of new schools and to a re-pairing of feeder schools to high school and the now junior high system. This upheaval and reshifting of the grandchild generation has led to increased mingling of former social classes and breaking of barriers.

The rulings on integration have continued to make the

social milieu of Gaston County a true democracy. Racial problems still exist but none of a major nature have ever erupted in open revolt. It is expected that Gastonia's next mayor will be a black who was also one of the first of his race ever to serve on a council of a Southern city.

A number of blacks have become members of white churches in the county (three Baptist churches). Blacks frequently visit the churches. Lately, church bus ministries are recruiting blacks for children's worship and Sunday School. To be sure, the presence of blacks in "all white" churches creates problems but cracks are appearing in the almost impenetrable color barrier to the socialization of an entire community. On the day that "Honey" King was gunned down by one of her own race in Atlanta, the first black children were being baptized in a formerly all white church.

Civic clubs, entertainment and recreation are aiding socialization in that people of all races, creeds and social status are meeting in non-combative areas and becoming friends.

Religious. Recently a map was prepared which locates three hundred and forty churches within Gaston County of all denominations and sects. This is almost one church for each square mile of land area! With a county population of 186,000 this is a ratio of one church to each 425 inhabitants and new churches are organized annually.

One half of the Gaston Baptist churches are under three hundred in membership. A recent estimate concludes that one of four persons in Gaston County is a member of a Baptist Church and that three of four live in a Baptist home.[15]

Other denominations by rank in numbers are Methodist,

Presbyterian, Lutheran, Church of God, Wesleyan, Catholic, Episcopal, a host of independents, sects and smaller groups. Belmont Abbey is the only Catholic Abbey in the United States. It was founded in 1876 in the wilderness of the area by a group of Benedictine Monks who came to establish a monastery. Following Vatican II, the first known Protestant-Catholic wedding took place in the Belmont Abbey Cathedral with my assisting in the ceremony.

Church plants in the area range in size and costs from an independent group meeting in an abandoned mill house to the multi-million dollar First Presbyterian Church of Gastonia built on the highest "flat land" in all the county. Baptist real estate holdings exceed twenty-five million dollars.[16] Annual receipts registered by these Baptist churches for 1974 were in excess of six million dollars.[17]

Each Gaston community has its own inter-denominational pastors' conference for planning limited ecumenical activity. In addition, these units frequently support in whole (or part) good government, morality, law enforcement, and honest elections, and take stands on varied social issues such as race, gambling, and legalized alcohol. A 1967 stand by Baptists, Wesleyans, Methodists, Church of God, and A. R. P.'s resulted in new voter registration and election procedures.

II. Origin, Organization and Growth

Origins. When the Elder Shubal Stearns came to North Carolina in 1758[18] and organized the Sandy Creek Missionary Baptist Association, Baptists were already worshiping in what is now Gaston County.

A two hundred year history of the Long Creek Memorial

Baptist Church[19] indicates that at the reorganization of the church in 1772 and the construction of its first building Baptists had been worshiping at Brush Arbor Church for some years.

Baptists in the county, therefore, have endured the siege of Indians; watched the birth of a nation; suffered the ravages of two major wars; felt the heel of the conqueror; groveled up through poverty to economic prosperity; been maligned publicly;[20] but stand today as the leading Christian denomination within the county.

Long Creek was at times a member of the Broad River, Kings Mountain and South Fork Baptist Associations. It was the only Baptist work in the area until Bruington Church (now Stanley First) was organized in 1853; Mt. Zion in 1859, and Sandy Plains in 1863. The Civil War and Sherman's march to the sea, which touched the area, impeded the spread of Baptist work in the county. Liston Pope points out still another factor for the slow growth of Baptists in the beginning but later rapid increase. He says that Baptists did not possess favored status or wealth and were generally discriminated against by their wealthier Presbyterian and Lutheran neighbors.[21]

However, following the Civil War and the coming of the textile mills, which caused a migration of the dispossessed and landless from the surrounding areas to the mill villages, Baptist work began to grow and in rapid order the following churches were organized: Hickory Grove, 1873; First, Belmont, 1874; First, Gastonia, 1876; Dallas, 1879; Shady Grove, 1881. By 1919, eighteen other Baptist churches had been organized in the territory called Gaston County.[22]

Organization. On Tuesday, November 4, 1919, at 10

o'clock A.M., delegates from twenty-six churches met together at First Baptist Church, Gastonia, and organized themselves into a new Baptist Association. Other churches not listed above and represented at the organizational meeting were: Alexis, Bessemer City (First), Cherryville (First), East Belmont, East Gastonia, High Shoals, Lucia, Loray, Lowell, Mayworth (now Cramerton First), McAdenville, Mt. Beulah, Mt. Holly (First), Ranlo, South Gastonia (now South Marietta St. Baptist), Spencer Mountain and Tuckaseegee.[23] All of these churches were within the county limits of Gaston County and remain members of the Association with the exception of the church at Lucia and Spencer Mountain. Lucia, in building their new building, moved into Lincoln County and joined fellowship with the South Fork Association. Spencer Mountain although giving the Association the record of its doctrinal beliefs, left the Association by default in 1974 because of doctrinal differences.

All the churches were received from either the South Fork or Kings Mountain Associations with the exception of Ranlo which was received as a newly organized church and Lucia. No mention is made of this church in the first *Annual* other than that it was struggling at the time and in need of financial help. However, Lucia, Ranlo and the others named became the Gaston County Baptist Association.[24]

Growth. The first *Annual* of the Association carries no statistical tables. A motion to include as information states, "... the statistical report of the churches forming the new association, are found in the minutes of the Kings Mountain and South Fork Association..." The 1920 *Annual* shows the membership to be 5,873. Excluding baptisms, letters, restorations and losses by letter, exclusions, death and the membership of two new churches (Calvary and Hull's Grove), the Association began with 5,211 members and twenty-six churches.

The growth of the Association has been phenomenal. Table V indicates the record at ten year intervals with the exception of the last period which simply brings the record to present date.[25]

It would be well to note from Table V that Baptist growth in the county increased in all areas of measurement until 1959 when a decline began in membership of all organizations except music.

Secondly, a huge building boom did not take place between 1969 and 1973. The $11,000,000 increase in value of church properties can largely be discounted as a tax re-evaluation.

It is interesting to note also that in 1920 *per capita* gifts were $26.07 with $10.99 going to missions (28% of total gifts to the $75 million campaign). In 1974, *per capita* gifts were $160.03 with $28.89 to missions (10% of total gifts to the Cooperative Program).

III. Purpose

At the first session of the Gaston County Baptist Association, pastors W. C. Barrett, F. M. Huggins, C. C. Kiser, D. F. Putnam and J. L. Vipperman were elected to draft a constitution and report to the next session.[26] The minutes of the second annual session, meeting with the Long Creek Memorial Baptist Church, do not include a motion for the adoption of the constitution but it appears on the inside of the front and back covers of the booklet.

TABLE V - GROWTH IN THE GASTON BAPTIST ASSOCIATION 1920 - 1974

Year No. Churches	1920 28	1929 36	1939 38	1949 56	1959 84	1969 90	1974 93
Membership	5,873	10,166	13,725	20,550	31,200	36,139	38,739
Baptisms	459	523	969	1,581	1,689	1,025	1,184
SS Enrolment	5,383	10,497	15,751	19,821	29,563	26,611	24,877
Ch. Trn.Enrol.	-0-	1,761	2,281	4,602	9,428	8,111	6,583
Music Enrol.	-0-	-0-	-0-	-0-	2,487	3,970	5,159
WMU Enrol.	-0-	1,317	2,464	4,619	6,457	5,351	5,446
Bro. Enrol.	-0-	-0-	-0-	445	2,422	2,057	2,825
Total Receipts	$153,107	126,921	163,711	884,780	1,817,378	3,443,878	6,199,535
Val. of Prop.	$348,414	1,042,416	1,014,865	2,626,804	9,244,283	16,507,929	25,054,517
Gifts to Missions	$ 61,602	36,057	35,756	160,610	354,843	672,739	1,032,566
Coop. Program	$ 42,369	13,923	16,365	93,483	243,371	428,536	601,372
Assoc. Missions	$ -0-	-0-	292	3,205	10,979	43,391	66,103
Home Missions	$ 3,983	10,339	361	2,926	8,603	29,099	42,934
For. Missions	$ 3,035	10,915	8,458	11,965	44,073	114,435	132,279
State Missions	$ 11,565	No report	6,194	41,812	34,564	46,734	68,387
Other Miss.	$ 650	880	1,456	7,219	13,253	10,544	65,872

It declares the purpose of the Association to be:

> It shall be the object of this Association to furnish the gospel (as we hold it) to the people within the bounds of the Association, and to cooperate with the Baptist State Convention of North Carolina and the Southern Baptist Convention in all the work of these conventions.[27]

The purpose was to evangelize Gaston County with the "Gospel as we hold it." The Philadelphia Confession of Faith was the statement of the "gospel as we hold it."[28] Another purpose was to cooperate with the Baptist State Convention of North Carolina and the Southern Baptist Convention. Apparently, cooperation meant support and prayerful concern. The Association, born during the Seventy-Five Million Campaign, reported $43,269.00 given to the campaign in 1920. Reports on all areas of state and Southern Baptist work are also included in this second Annual.[29] The success of the Association's "furnishing the gospel" can be measured by a net gain of 662 members after its first year. Of these 459 were by baptism. The Association also gained two newly organized churches. By 1929, the church membership and Sunday School enrollment had doubled and an additional eight churches had been added to its membership.[30]

During its Silver Anniversary meeting, 1943, a move was made to employ a full time Associational Missionary. Conversation with some ministers who were present at the meeting, now retired in this area, reveals that this motion and its adoption led some of the brethren to believe that a new constitution would be necessary.[31] A committee was named. It included: J. A. Snow, B. A. Bowers, T. L. Cashwell, and a layman, David P. Dellinger, long-time Associational Clerk.

Their short-lived constitution reported the purposes to be:

> We, the Missionary Baptist Churches of CHRIST-JESUS composing the Gaston Baptist Association, convinced of the necessity of an association of churches in order to perpetuate fellowship among us and better the cause of CHRIST-JESUS, do hereby agree and subscribe to the following rules.[32]

The Reverend T. L. Cashwell, Sr., said that the committee's work was misunderstood in dropping the word "county" from the Association's name and also in failing to spell out what they meant by "better the cause of CHRIST-JESUS."[33] The bone of contention, however, was not their failing to spell out the later meaning but the dropping of "county," from the official name of the Association.[34]

The Executive Committee, sensing the discontent among the pastors, requested the Reverend P. A. Hicks, pastor of the East Belmont Church, to revise or rewrite a constitution: to present it to the Pastors' Conference for discussion and suggested changes; to bring it to the Executive Committee for study, and then present it to the Association at its next annual session.[35]

Mr. Hicks did his homework well. His one man constitution was presented to the 27th Annual Session in 1945 and it passed without discussion or known murmur.

The purpose projected in the constitution of 1945 remains the same today. However, the portion in italics was added in a revision of 1964. This addition tells the "who" of cooperation.

We, the Missionary Baptist Churches of Jesus Christ, composing the Gaston Baptist Association, convinced of the necessity of an association of churches in order to promote fellowship, missions, education, Christian service, the preaching of the gospel, and to cooperate with the *Baptist State Convention of North Carolina and the Southern Baptist Convention* in their work, do hereby agree and subscribe to the following articles.[36]

The purposes as now stated in the constitution of the Association are six: The promotion of fellowship, missions, education, Christian service, preaching of the gospel and cooperation with the North Carolina Baptist State Convention and the Southern Baptist Convention.[37]

Fellowship. Murray Ross includes in his use of the term "community" those "groups of people who share some common interest or function, such as welfare, agriculture, education, religion."[38] His use of the word "community" approximates the meaning of *tesumeth yad* in Leviticus 6:2 and *koinonia* as used in Acts 2:42. It means the same thing as the term fellowship as defined by Gaston Baptists, "to deal with or to be together and to actively participate in areas of common interest."

Missions. Lloyd Corder defines an association as "a fellowship of churches on mission in their setting."[39] To be on mission to Gaston Baptists means to be an *apostolos* or *martus* to the work and witness of Jesus Christ wherever one can witness personally or make it possible for others to do so.

Education. Gaston Baptists have supported education both public and private since their organization. In 1919, the Association adopted the Boiling Springs Academy (Gardner-Webb College) as its institution.[40] Every subsequent report shows continuing support of cooperating institutions.

The Reverend M.L. Barnes stated in his report on education to the Seventh Annual Session of the Association:

> The life of a nation depends upon its schools. The value of a school depends upon its ideals. The ideals of a school have their highest worth only as they are Christian. It is the duty of the churches to make these ideals dominant in education.[41]

The work of Gaston Baptists in the field of education has been to this end. Largely composed of unlearned "mill hands" in origin, Baptists hailed the compulsory education laws passed in the 1920's in North Carolina.[42] Many public schools were established in the mill villages and received the support of Baptist Churches already at work nearby. Today the children of the founders, now young professionals, and the grandchildren serve in churches with the old timers who spent little or no time in public schools but whose love and labor for the Lord led them to believe in education.[43]

Christian Service. Service to be Christian must be done in the name of Christ. Gaston Baptists have believed this from the time of their organization and also that it must be done in secret. This later belief led researcher, Liston Pope, ten years after the Loray strike, to believe that Baptists did nothing to alleviate the suffering of the strikers and their families.[44] Upon interviewing several members of two churches concerning this matter, all of them looked at me as if I had lost my mind. Their answers ranged from, "Pastor, don't we help now?", to "You know we did!" Each answer was given in a voice of reproach. Looking back over eight years as pastor in the community referred to in footnote 43, I know that during this period a committee of five persons handled the matters of Christian necessities of life to those in need of them and that this committee kept no record of its activities. However, hundreds of dollars, food, clothing and other necessities were distributed across these years. Questioning five pastors of other Baptist Churches, I find this to have been standard policy through the years.[45]

This is the spirit which led Gaston Baptists to pioneer in Christian Social Ministries. In 1965, the Association began a Mission Center in connection with the Temple Baptist Church and has expanded the beginning volunteer ministry to include a full time Director of Christian Social Ministries and a full time Case Worker. This service is still being carried on without trumpets in the Gaston Community.

Preaching the Gospel. The heralding of the good news has been such a part of the Gaston Baptist Association's work and emphasis in its ministry, it passes with no comment other than that proclamation is carried on from the pulpit, personal witness, teaching, education, and Christian social ministries.

Cooperation. From the beginning of the Association Gaston Baptists emphasized the competency of each believer. It would be well if each individual believer could be independent of all others but this is not practical. It is the ideal but leads to monasticism. The practical is cooperation and is best described by the word synergy from the Greek work *sunergos* — "being a together worker." The scriptures will show that each church is autonomous but that it exists in fellowships brought together by the Holy Spirit (1 Cor. 3:16 and 6:19ff.). The scripture also shows the churches acting independently but also cooperatively (2 Cor. 8-9 and Acts 15). In each instance the Lord's will was sought and the church acted in a democratic manner under this leadership of Christ.

This is the kind of action according to Matthew 18:19-20, which has the assurance of the presence of Christ with us.

Insistence upon autonomy at the expense of cooperative missions will cause tensions. Such tensions are created when there is a lack of knowledge that a church is free to make its own decisions only as it focuses on the authority of God and the lordship of Christ. This focus will prevent isolation and individualism and lead to working together in the body of Christ. When the Holy Spirit animates the church, the church and/or other body will focus on mission rather than maintenance. It will be a fellowship working together with God. Gaston Baptists have followed this practical application of the gospel across the years but in recent times my cursory research has led to a belief there is a need for in-depth research and a strategy planned for renewing this spirit of cooperation.

Chapter II of this work will seek to translate the purposes of the association into measureable objectives. Then an analysis will be made of the Gaston Baptist

Association in relation to the accomplishment of its objectives, a decade of mission giving, and factors sought which might have led to a decline in the spirit of cooperation as referred to above.

DETERMINING CAUSAL FACTORS IN DECLINE

In the preceding chapter I have sought to show the background heritage of today's Gaston Baptists. This heritage is the frame on which they will continue to spin out their threads of purpose and their mission. In a sense, Gaston Baptists have become heirs of their own labors and are becoming ancestors of their continuing future.

Have they succeeded in their purpose? Is their present a fulfilment of their past? Will their future be more fruitful in carrying out their mission? The answers to these questions will be sought in this chapter.

I. Purposes Stated As Objectives

It is common knowledge that researchers disagree on which can best be measured: purpose or objective. I will assume the latter and seek to state purpose as objective. Then the objectives will be measured by my research and the research of thirty-five pastors who responded to a work session and questionnaire related to mission gifts and to the strengths and weaknesses of the Association. A copy of the questionnaire is appended.

The objectives are as follows:

Fellowship. To promote a feeling for each other within the individual fellowships which would engender a spirit of cooperation among the churches to share of the same spirit in spreading the gospel beyond their walls.

Missions. To promote the sharing of the whole gospel of

Christ in all the world.

Education. To promote Christian education through Sunday Schools and Baptist schools and colleges.

Christian Service. To promote a service to mankind on behalf of Christ which would provide the necessities of life to those in need of them.

Preaching. To promote the preaching of the good news concerning Jesus through the establishment of new churches and missions and through encouraging pastors to gospel preaching.

Cooperation. To work together with the Baptist State Convention of North Carolina and the Southern Baptist Convention in aiding the churches in producing the best possible atmosphere in which each child of God might develop to full usefulness in the service of Christ.

II. Investigating the Record of Missions Gifts

Research by the Director of Missions. After two years on the job, the present Director of Missions prepared a ten year chart on the work of the Association. The chart included factors such as baptisms, membership, organizational membership and average attendance, gifts to churches, church gifts to missions and others. Analyzation of the chart showed increases and continuing growth in organizational strength, membership, gifts to the churches and *dollars* to missions.

However, one startling fact surfaced in the survey. Although the Association was contributing more dollars to missions than any other North Carolina association (it took pride in the fact because it was not most numerous in Baptists or monetary potential), it had declined in

TABLE V I

A Ten Year Study of Mission Gifts from Member Churches of the Gaston Baptist Association

Item	1963	1972	% Change	10 Year Total
1. Baptisms	987	1,178	19.4	11,201
2. Resident Members	26,747	30,493	14.0	30,493
3. Total Members	32,797	37,074	13.0	37,074
4. Total Receipts	2,192,210	4,058,094	85.0	30,626,322
5. Total Salaries	612,106	1,184,461	93.5	8,499,008
6. New Construction	226,155	382,045	68.9	6,514,266
7. Church Missions	54,336	46,735	40.0	362,558
8. Cooperative Program	319,949	512,703	60.2	4,094,632
9. Associational Missions	15,424	60,924	294.9	334,833
10. State Missions	5,811	9,494	63.3	79,212
11. Annie Armstrong	15,005	36,838	145.5	244,009
12. Lottie Moon	68,891	106,738	54.9	955,605
13. Christian Education	5,209	10,146	94.8	89,510
14. Children's Home	13,208	18,472	39.9	147,448
15. Hospital	6,486	12,281	89.3	89,664
16. Homes for Aging	2,968	6,466	117.9	42,951
17. All Other	6,994	39,149	*	143,706
18. Grand Total Missions	514,281	859,946	67.2	6,584,128
Mission % of Total Rcpts	23.5	21.2	-2.3	21.5
Coop. % of Total Rcpts	14.6	12.6	-2.0	13.4
Coop. % of Mission Total	62.2	59.6	-2.6	62.2
Annie A. % of Receipts	.7	.9	+.2	.8
Annie A. % of Missions	2.9	4.3	+1.4	3.7
L. Moon % of Receipts	3.1	2.6	-.5	3.1
L. Moon % of Missions	13.4	12.4	-1.0	14.5
Local Mission and All Other	2.8	2.1	-.7	1.7
L. Mission, etc. % Missions	11.9	9.9	-2.0	7.7
State Desig % Receipts	1.5	1.4	-.1	1.5
State Desig % Missions	6.5	6.6	.1	6.8
Assoc. % of Receipts	.7	1.5	.8	1.2
Assoc. % of Missions	3.0	7.1	4.1	5.5

*Items 17 and 7 are included together in the 40% increase listed opposite Item 7 because of the way in accounting for local mission expenditures which took place in the Associational Annuals during this ten years.

percentage gifts to missions and gifts through the Cooperative Program of missions: Total receipts had increased 85% in ten years, but total gifts to all missions had declined 2.3% and gifts to cooperative missions had declined by 2%. If the percentages given to missions had been maintained throughout the ten year period, $613,058 more would have been given for this cause. If that percentage amount had been added to gifts given and the Cooperative Missions percentage of total mission gifts had been maintained (and it was), $381,322 more would have been given through Cooperative Missions.[1]

To the casual observer it would seem that, gauged by the dollar mark, the Association was reaching its objectives of Fellowship, Mission and Cooperation. But the researcher could tell from these percentage declines, that eyes had turned inward and that in the area of mission gifts there was multiple failure in achieving objectives. Curiosity and the belief this area was in the greater need of probing, led me to prepare an in-depth table on Mission Gifts.

Possible causal factors for decline identified. A number of factors, which may have contributed to the percentage decline in mission gifts by member churches of the Gaston Baptist Association, come immediately to light when the table is studied.

1. Salaries increased from $612,106 annually to $1,184,461, an increase of 94%.

2. New construction averaged $651,426 per year. This is a yearly average increase of 188% over 1963.

3. Associational Mission Gifts increased 294% from $15,424 to $60.924.

4. Gifts to State, Home, Foreign and Designated Missions increased 1066%.

Doubtless these are dominant factors in the percentage decline in mission gifts but will be researched further and verified.

Pastor's research. In order to determine why the condition of decline existed, the Director invited all the pastors of the Association to work sessions. At the session they were to prepare a table similar to Table VI, but on their church only. Forty-four pastors responded. Their response produced an exceptional random sampling not only of the entire Association but of the groups within the geographical divisions of the Association's land area as well. This is reflected in Table VII, pages 32 and 33.

Many pastors attending had done organizational studies of a similar nature but not one had ever studied the record of his church's mission gifts' record. Their comments ranged from "You've got to be kidding," "Something's wrong with the figures," to "I am embarrassed!"

Possible factors for decline identified by pastors. Their comments during the work session and continuing interviews revealed another dominant factor in decline. They simply were not aware that a dollars increase did not always mean an increase in mission support when viewed through percentages!

Following the completion and study of their tables, the pastors were asked to complete the questionnaire (Appendix II) regarding the work session, their findings and for introspective answers to the question, "Why decline?"

Every one of them confirmed the four factors which I identified and added those which follow. The number appearing after the factor is the number of pastors who identified the factor.

1. The Sunday School Board's Genesis Commentary and

TABLE VII

Causal Factors Verified

CHURCH and GROUP		Resident Mem. '72	Dollars Coop. '63	Gifts Coop. '72	Dollars Missions '63	Gifts Missions '72	Pastor's Comments on Decline
GROUP I							
Berea	(1)	170	374.	900.+	856.	2,711.+	
Catawba Heights	(1)	555	530.	5,486.+	981.	7,896.+	
McAdenville	(3)	438	2,214.	1,000.+	4,293.	8,636.-	% not kept in mind
Mount Holly 1st	(1)	712	21,623.	27,402.-	26,086.	41,369.+	Local exp. increased
Lakeview	(2)	136	130.	660.+	239.	1,579.+	
		2,011	24,871	35,448.	32,455.	62,191.	
GROUP II							
Belmont, 1st.	(2)	878	19,573.	27,437.-	30,623.	48,086.+	Emphasized specials
Belmont, East	(1)	628	7,500.	11,040.+	11,198.	18,348.+	New Staff Member
Cramerton, 1st.	(3)	465	9,917.	14,302.+	14,793.	21,477.-	Liberalism-Commentary
Cramerton, West	(3)	237	598.	100.-	1,153.	2,394.+	Liberalism-Baptism Issue
Riverside	(2)	176	123.	0.-	470.	3,790.+	Bldg. Program
Sandy Plains	(2)	700	17,795.	20,671.+	11,339.	27,064.-	Pastoral Changes
South Point	(4)	141	3,130.	1,258.+	4,228.	2,158.-	
		3,225	58,636.	75,308.	73,809.	123,317.	
GROUP III							
Long Creek	(2)	567	6,300.	8,000.-	8,700.	21,577.-	Local needs
New Life	(4)	208	1,251.	2,429.-	1,674.	4,005.-	Liberalism-Baptism Issue
Spencer Mtn.	(1)	317	0.	0.-	131.	0.-	Commentary-Liberalism
Stanley, 1st.	(2)	708	18,612.	20,502.+	25,301.	30,289.+	Local Needs
		1,800	26,163.	30,931.	35,806.	56,372.	
GROUP IV							
Anthony Grove	(2)	180	0.	1,895.+	89.	3,041.+	
Cherryville 1st.	(2)	1,405	15,570.	32,000.+	19,264.	44,477.+	
Mt. Beulah	(2)	314	483.	6,488.+	949.	9,806.+	
Sunnyside	(3)	92	0.	0.-	131.	400.+	Pastoral Turnover
Shady Grove	(2)	385	4,462.	10,920.+	5,450.	15,108.+	
		2,376	20,515.	51,303.	25,883.	72,832.	

Church		1	2	3	4	Notes
GROUP V						
Bessemer C. 1st	(1)	850	9,836.	11,024.-	13,648.	17,100.-	Local needs
Bessemer C. 2nd	(6)	68	573.	0.-	625.	5,471.+	2 Indpend. former pastors
Holland Mem.	(3)	136	150.	120.+	222.	563.+	
Chestnut Ridge	(2)	185	0.	3,914.+	68.	5,064.+	
		1,239	10,559.	15,058.	14,563.	28,198.	
GROUP VI						
Chapel Grove	(2)	333	408.	4,804.+	762.	7,315.+	Emphasized specials
Cleveland Hts.	(3)	74	0.	447.+	36.	1,104.+	
Loray	(2)	944	18,000.	20,898.-	26.968.	34,620.-	
Unity	(2)	1,010	10,001.	26,120.+	12,848.	32,395.+	
W. Franklin	(3)	340	2,720.	5,038.+	4,187.	7,552.+	
		2,701	31,129.	57,307.	44,801.	82,993.	
GROUP VII						
Bethany	(2)	141	156.	100.+	356.	600.+	Balanced giving
Calvary	(3)	319	190.	3,407.+	1,013.	5,032.+	% not kept in mind
Gastonia,1st.	(2)	1,558	35,496.	45,075.-	51,294.	95,699.-	Local needs
Love Mem.	(1)	430	2,000.	2,400.-	2,860.	4,903.+	
S. Marietta	(4)	631	2,422.	7,000.+	5,299.	10,524.+	
Victory	(2)	541	7,424.	8,100.-	8,294.	9,875.-	
		3,620	47,688.	66,082.	69,116.	126,638.	
GROUP VIII						
Gastonia, East	(2)	948	10,345.	15,102.-	42,308.	28,864.-	Bldg. and new staff
Flint-Groves	(3)	1,015	16,721.	17,000.-	20,424.	20,242.-	Staff increased
Fraley	(2)	146	(166) 312.	150.-	511.	519.-	Local expense
Lowell, 1st.	(3)	450	4,610.	5,229.-	6,864.	6,830.-	Pastor turnover
Parkwood	(1)	473	(1632,923.	6,199.-	5,902.	13,508.-	Designations-Specials
Ranlo	(2)	553	4,700.	6,500.-	5,776.	14,260.+	Emphasized specials1
Woodlawn	(2)	465	4,021.	3,900.-	4,903.	7,559.-	Bldgs burned-replaced
New Hope	(1)	264	942.	3,091.+	2,276.	4,806.+	
		4,314	44,574.	57,171.	89,364.	96,588.	
Grand Totals		21,286	264,135.	388,608.	385,797.	649,129.	
% of Assoc. Total		69.8	82.6	75.8	83.4	76.6	

44 Churches participated in the Chart Survey. (46.8%)
35 Pastors completed the questionnaire. (41.2%)
+ or - in Dollars columns indicate a percentage increase or decrease over 1963.
(1) Number indicates number of pastors in ten years covered.

subsequent SBC controversy. (4)

2. The push of denominational agencies and Boards for *their* special offerings. (35)

3. Failure to promote the Cooperative Program. (26)

4. Doctrinal controversy in North Carolina over baptism. (35)

5. Undoubted liberalism of Southern Baptist Seminary professors and North Carolina Baptist College teachers. (11)

6. Growth of independent, designated giving to other than SBC missions. (13)

7. Increase in local mission expenditure and ministries. (7)

8. Turnover in pastors. (5)

III. Causal Factors Verified

Increases in other mission gifts. In listing possible causal factors of decline, I identified two major contributing facts as "Gifts to State, Home, Foreign and Designated Mission Increases" of 1066% in dollars amounts and "Associational Mission Gifts" increases in dollars amounts of 294%. The pastors identified: The Special Offerings Push, Growth of Independent and Designated Giving, and Growth in Local Missions Expenditures. Each of these is reflected in Table VII, on the previous pages.

Frank L. Perry[2] in writing about the rate of giving to the Cooperative Program, Lottie Moon Christmas Offering and Annie Armstrong Easter Offering said that the Cooperative Program increased 69.180%, while Lottie Moon and Annie Armstrong increased at 98.155 and 109.754 percent respectively. Earlier, Mr. Perry had argued[3] that lack of space devoted toward motivating gifts to the Cooperative Program in *The Commission* and *Home Missions*, while at the same time lavishing space on motivation for the special offering related to these journals, was responsible for this condition. Mr. Perry concluded:

> The facts seem to indicate that the rate of increase of special offerings correlates highly with the amount of space given in agency publications to the promotion of such offerings.[4]

And, my belief is that Mr. Perry implied the lack of space given to the Cooperative Program would account in part for the less rapid rate of increase of gifts to the Cooperative Program.

"The Report of the Study Committee of Fifteen to the Executive Committee of the SBC," given December 21, 1973, indicates on page 13, item 2, that "The Board" (Foreign) should more adequately promote the Cooperative Program," and on page 20, item 9, indicates that the Home Mission Board also is remiss in its duty to promote the Cooperative Program on an equal basis with the Annie Armstrong Offerings. A friend who attended the discussion of the Report has advised that discussion of these two matters centered on a supposed over-emphasis in the journals of these respective boards on their special offerings and not adequately covering the part of the Cooperative Program in their total work.

Following these leads, I made an intensive study of the *Cumulative Index to Articles in Sunday School Periodicals 1962-64* and *Southern Baptist Periodical Index 1965 through 1971*.[5] These indices index eighteen publications of the Sunday School Board, seven of Woman's Missionary Union, six of the Brotherhood, eleven of the Seminaries, and one each of the following: Executive Committee, Home Mission Board, Foreign Mission Board, Baptist Joint Committee on Public Affairs, Annuity Board, Education Commission, and Baptist Historical Commission. A total of forty-nine publications of Southern Baptists are then referenced in these works.

If Dr. Perry's and the Committee of Fifteen's conclusions were true,[6] then the total picture of "space given" correlating highly in increase of special offerings with space given, the ratio would be Cooperative Program 111, Annie Armstrong 40, and Lottie Moon 55 across the ten year period studied.

The Home Board carried twelve articles on the Cooperative Program and ten on the Annie Armstrong Offering in the period studied. The Foreign Board carried six articles on the Cooperative Program and nine on the Lottie Moon Offering. In all one hundred eleven articles were carried in publications indexed on the Cooperative Program, and 95 on both special offerings. If increase correlated highly on space given, the Cooperative Program would be ahead. Such is not the case!

It would seem that Dr. Perry and the Committee of Fifteen, as I and a host of Gaston Baptist pastors, were too much taken by the percentage rate of dollars increase and did not consider the percent of total receipts of each of these important offerings.

When these percentages are considered within the Gaston Baptist Association, increases in specials, associational gifts, offering push and growth of designated giving and local missions, prove to be no factors at all in the decline of gifts to missions.

TABLE VIII

Summary of Number of Articles Published in
Southern Baptist Publications Motivating Gifts to
the Cooperative Program
1962 - 1971

	1962	1963	1964	1965	1966	1967	1968	1969	1970	1971	10 Yr. Total
S.S.Bd.	1	5	0	1	2	2	1	0	0	0	12
Exec.C.		(Not		2	3	4	5	4	5	5	28
W.M.U.				19	3	5	6	1	4	5	43
Bro.		indexed)		4	1	0	3	0	0	0	8
Hm.Bd.				5	0	0	3	2	1	1	12
For.B.				0	0	4	1	1	0	0	6
Other				0	1	1	0	0	0	0	2
Totals	1	5	0	31	10	16	19	8	10	11	111

TABLE IX

Summary of Number of Articles Published in
Southern Baptist Publications Motivating Gifts to
the Special Offerings
1965 - 1971

	1965 AA	1965 LM	1966 AA	1966 LM	1967 AA	1967 LM	1968 AA	1968 LM	1969 AA	1969 LM	1970 AA	1970 LM	1971 AA	1971 LM	Totals AA	Totals LM
W.M.U.	6	4	7	9	1	3	5	1	5	11	4	7	2	5	30	40
Hm.Bd.	1		2				1		3				3		10	
For.Bd.				3		1								5		9
Bro.						1		2								3
S.S.Bd.						1										1
Exec.C.												2				2
Totals	7	4	9	12	1	6	6	3	8	11	4	9	5	10	40	55

Table VII, page 32 and 33, shows an increase in dollars gifts to the Cooperative Program and also Missions. Most, however, show a decline in percentage of total receipts going for these purposes.

Table VI, page 29, depicts the negating of the factors as above in clearer light. The numbered section of the table shows the comparison of dollars and the percent of dollars increase in ten years. It looks good and immediately the conclusion is erroneously reached as per the prior confession.

The bottom half of Table VI, page 24, places the matter in perspective:

Annie Armstrong	+ .2	Lottie Moon	- .5
Associational Missions	+ .8	Local & Designated	- .7
	+ 1.0	State	- .1
	- 1.3		- 1.3
	- .3		
Cooperative Program	- 2.0		
Missions % of Total	- 2.3		

Therefore, this group of factors cannot be verified as factors of decline within the Association. The 2.3% decline simply did not go to other missions!

Local church increase factors. The second set of possible factors consist of Salary and Staff increases, New Construction and one factor not previously mentioned: an increase in Other Local Expense. These may be best verified by simple arithmetic using statistics from Table VI, page 29.

	1963	1972
Salaries	612,106	1,184,461
New Construction	226,155	382,045
Missions	514,281	859,946
	1,352,542	2,426,452
Total Receipts	2,192,210	4,058,094

Other Local Expense	839,668	1,631,642
% Loc. Exp. of Tot. Receipts	38.3	40.2

```
                        40.2
                      - 38.3
Local Expense         + 1.9
Salaries              + 1.3
New Construction      -  .9
                      + 2.3
```

In comparing this sum with the sum of percentage decline in mission gifts, the factor of increase in Staff and Salaries is verified along with the new factor of Increase in Local Expense. However, New Construction proves to be no factor in the decline of mission gifts within the Gaston Baptist Association. One pastor said it succinctly, "Larger staff; larger salaries; greater overhead expense."[7]

The research team of Johnson and Cornell verified this same factor as the prime cause of cut back to missions in their study of churches of fifteen different major denominations in the United States and Canada:

The main thesis seemed to be that church people, to a jolting extent, had turned their interests away from the broader church labors to concentrate their resources more heavily on their home parishes. "Expenditures for local operations are at a level never before equaled in the history of the church."[8]

Gaston Baptists, it seems, are not unlike the sheep in other folds. The question remains, however, how did Missionary Baptists permit the 2.3% decline?

The remaining factors. Probably the greater factor is the hang up with dollars increase without increasing the dollars enough to maintain the percentage of total receipts ratio. A study of the full table prepared by the Superintendent but not included with this paper reveaals this gentle erosion across ten years.

Failure to promote the Cooperative Program has proved already to be no factor when compared with promotion of the special offerings. However, a study of Table VIII, page 37, will show that most promotion by Southern Baptist Convention agencies or boards is done with pastors and church leadership. Only the *Baptist Bulletin Service* reaches the people with Cooperative Program information with any regularity and/or punch. The *Biblical Recorder* (North Carolina Baptists' State paper) boasts of 110,000 circulation. It carries pertinent information relative to missions and the Cooperative Program. If every copy went to a North Carolina Baptist family, only one of five Baptists in the State would have it available for reading.

Consider the limited and declining circulations of *Home Missions, The Commission* and other Southern Baptist publications among the 10,000,000+ Southern Baptists and the charge "Lack of promotion of the Cooperative Program" will hold: not because it isn't tried but because the task is virtually impossible! This fact is well verified in the overall tone of the Committee of Fifteen's Report.

The publication of the Broadman Commentary on Genesis and resultant furor at the Southern Baptist Convention at Denver, 1970, led two pastors of the

Association to return to their churches denouncing the Southern Baptist Convention and its liberalism. Both churches eventually withdrew from the fellowship of all Baptist bodies and have become independent (individualistic is a better term).

Both of these pastors continue to denounce Southern Baptists from pulpit and airways and have had telling effect on four more of the member churches of the Gaston Baptist Association. This cost the Cooperative Program .2% in total of receipts, or $4,000 in known decline stemming from this issue.[9]

Liberalism in Our Schools and Colleges. This perennial issue is closely coupled with the above issue and played its part in decline as well. Four pastors (personal interviews) attributed the decline to Cooperative Program from their churches to this cause. The resultant loss in dollars was $4,578 or an additional .2%.

Doctrinal Issue on Baptism. This issue claimed prominence in the North Carolina Baptist State Convention compounded with the two issues just discussed, only confirmed the opinions of those pastors who had led their churches to Cooperative Program decreases in their opinions. Seven other pastors (five in interview; two by questionnaire) attributed the decline registered by their churches to this issue. In amount it was $3,022 or .3%.[10] Actually, this issue did not cost the Cooperative Program as much in cutting off funds as it did in some of the churches not giving normal increases to the Cooperative Program across 1971, 1972 and 1973. As one pastor, whose church showed no decrease, said, "Some of us are disturbed by the positions state leaders have taken on this baptism question."[11] If one half the decline could be attributed to this attitude, which is held by many, it would account for an additional $2,750.

At this point the percentage decline can be attributed as follows:

Commentary	—	.2
Liberalism	—	.2
Baptismal Issue	—	.3
Attitudes	—	.6
	—	1.3

The remaining 1% would necessarily then be attributed to the remaining factors of decline which were discovered: a lack of awareness that increase in dollars did not mean an increase in mission support when viewed through percentages[12] and to the rapid turnover of pastors.[13]

Only five of the forty-four churches included in Table VII show a decline in dollars amounts to missions, but seventeen show a decline in percentages.[14] Of the seventeen showing decline, fourteen had more than one pastor during the period. A study of individual church charts shows the lack of pastoral leadership during these thirty-six turnovers, to be costly to mission gifts, both in percentage of total receipts and dollars amounts.

IV. Summary of Factors Verified

The factors verified as causal factors in the decline of percentage gifts to missions in the Gaston Baptist Association are:

1. Publication of the *Broadman Commentary* and resultant furor.

2. Liberalism in colleges and seminaries.

3. Baptismal issue in North Carolina.

4. Pastor resentment of position taken by denominational mission leaders in the State on baptism.

5. Erosion of percentage of total receipts going to missions — obscured by increase in dollars amounts.

6. Pastoral turnover.

It may be admitted at this point that, as Dr. Perry pointed out[15] and the Committee of Fifteen surmised, the Annie Armstrong Offering in dollars amounts increased more rapidly than the dollars increase to the Cooperative Program. However, in the Gaston Baptist Association this increase is to be attributed to the Home Board's entering into a cooperative agreement with the North Carolina Baptist State Convention and the Gaston Baptist Association to enter into a Christian Social Ministries Program in the Association in 1968. The Annie Armstrong Offering in the Spring of 1969 amounted to 4.2% of total gifts to missions and had increased .1% to 1972. The total mission gifts of -2.3% may then be accounted for as follows:

Coop. % of Missions	- 2.6	Annie Arm. % of Miss.	+ 1.4
Lottie Moon	- 1.0	State Design.	.1
Local Missions	- 2.0	Assoc.	4.1
	5.6		5.6

These figures indicate the percentage decline to the Cooperative Program, Lottie Moon and Local Missions programs was picked up by Annie Armstrong, State Missions and Associational Missions. The 2.3% decline was actually a decline in dollars to all missions and as previously discussed was claimed by Local Expense and Salaries.

It is obvious that the 1963 Associational Missions gifts

of $15,424[16] is a figure unsuitable for supporting an Associational Missions program. Nor is the figure of 1972, $60,924, adequate for the needs of the Association.

When the past of the Association is known[17] and its present decline in gifts to missions and the reasons for it have been declared (as in this chapter), it seems to me that three choices are open to the Association at this point:

1. Forget our common heritage of belief that each believer is a priest under God and, therefore, trust no one but ourselves, cut off mission support, withdraw into our local churches and die together; or to

2. Let our culture and our peers so influence us to preserve our cultural heritage and its institution that we will not move beyond the barriers which we have erected against the onslaught of supposed untruth with the real values which have been entrusted to us as THE CHURCH; or to

3. Plan change which will help us to overcome errors and mistrusts of the past and get on with doing *our* part on mission in our setting. We are convinced with the Committee of Fifteen, "That in many areas most people want change, but that the democratic defense of minority interests too often inhibits general change."[18]

A STRATEGY FOR INCREASE

Before beginning an attack on the causes for decline in mission gifts to cooperative missions from member churches of the Gaston Baptist Association, it would be well to assess the strengths and weaknesses of the Association. In so doing, the agent of change will be in a better position to plan a strategy to counter opposing forces and causes of decline.

Strengths and Weaknesses of the Association

Strengths. The pastors were asked in the questionnaire, "What do you consider to be the strengths of the Association? It's weaknesses?" A number of laymen were also asked these questions and the following summarizes the consensus of opinion of both groups.

1. Order (Administration)
2. Organization[1]
3. Personnel
4. Diversified Programming and proper promotion
5. Fellowship (koinonia)
6. Dedicated laymen and pastors
7. Desire for unity and prayerful concern for each other
8. Associational program of Christian Social Ministries
9. No hierarchy of concern on part of the Director
10. Loyalty to Association's Articles of Faith[2]

To these may be added the Association's enviable record of being "No. 1" in mission gifts among the State's associations. To remain in this spot gives as much spirit and unity to the Association as it does to a winning college and its team.[3]

Weaknesses. The pastors and laymen pulled no punches in listing those things which they thought to be weaknesses of the Association.

1. Pettiness of "picky pastors" who tend to criticize but not constructively

2. Evangelism record weak

3. Tendency on part of some to raise public objections to cooperative missions but fail to attend programs and meetings which might open "closed minds"

4. Failure to show enough loving concern between churches and pastors in crisis times — church and/or personal

5. Not enough information distributed of a testimonial nature concerning mission work

6. Overlapping church fields and bus ministries

7. Refusal on part of some pastors to support the whole Cooperative Program when a denominational official's doctrinal position runs counter to what "they" believe to be the Baptist Faith and Message.

8. Layman disinterest

9. Poor programs, sometimes

An Assessment. It is apparent that as both lists are compared that some items in each list counter those in the other. Still others confirm causes of decline already verified. Many of the weaknesses listed provide clues to further studies which should be made in connection with the mission of the Association. The weaknesses and strengths may be paired as follows:

Weaknesses	Strengths to Overcome
1. Those which show a lack of knowledge and/or training of pastors – Numbers, 1, 3, 7	Numbers, 2, 4, 7, 9
2. Those which show a lack of knowledge and/or training of laymen – Numbers 4, 5, 8, 9	Numbers 1, 2, 4, 6, 8
3. Those which show a need for outreach – Numbers 2, 6.	Numbers 3, 5, 8, 10

These may be placed into the planned strategy as: (1) Overcoming error with truth; (2) Attacking unknowing with knowledge; and (3) Absorbing individualism into community.

Other Strategies

In Chapter Three, Causal factors of decline were verified.[4] The first three listed fit well into the strategies as above. However, the pastors' resentment of denominational leaders will require a special strategy and will be dealt with first.

The percentage erosion factor will be handled as: Countering inequities with fair share. I feel that the sixth verified factor, Pastoral Turnover, will heal itself as the Strategy for Increase is applied and the minister comes to a greater sense of security and purpose in his present pastorate.

The Strategy for Increase

Overcome resentment with love. One major factor for decline has been the pastors' resentment of denominational officials whose opinions differed from "the faith once delivered."[5] and the apparent lack of understanding on the part of denominational officials of the pastors' position. One pastor said, "They just don't care about us!"[6] Another pastor in answering the question "Do you have a personal objection to a Board, etc.?" replied, "I have voiced my objection through the years to the right people. They always smile and assure me of their concern, and things that are bad today just get worse."[7]

I am well aware that a Secretary (or any official of any Convention) is only one man but his contacts with the churches of his Convention are made through the pastor. Johnson and Cornell[8] in their study show the pastor to be the key person in the denominational process. It is through him the denomination hears from the churches and the churches hear from the denomination. If he be this important, then one of the first duties of a denominational official should be to know, to hear, to seek to understand and to guide pastors on mission in their settings. Theirs is a joint task and complete understanding is necessary.

Pastors in general feel that failure to cooperate completely and follow the "party line" ostracizes them in the views of those desiring cooperation. This feeling is engendered by officials who too often react quickly to criticisms without understanding first the true intent of the question. In my ministry as a pastor, I have had several exchanges with such luminaries as James L. Sullivan, Albert McLellan, O.T. Binkley and the late W.C. Reed. Each question was voiced with a desire to give helpful information, but each reply was a squelch based on obvious oversight of material included in my inquiry. However high their hackles rose, all but the inquiry to W.C. Reed, have resulted in desired changes. How much my inquiries affected the changes only eternity can tell and I suffered hurt feelings only for a little while.

Currently, Southern Baptists are beset with the growing

Baptist Faith and Message group and their *Southern Baptist Journal* publication. It began with a request from M.O. Owens, Jr., Gastonia, N.C., asking that the Executive Committee of the Southern Baptist Convention print a reply article in *The Southern Baptist Program* to William Hull's "Is the Bible Infallible?" Mr. Owens' request was refused. He took his request to the Southern Baptist Convention at Philadelphia in 1973 and was immediately attacked by Duke McCall as presenting the most vicious attack ever heard on the convention floor. Both McLellan and McCall missed Mr. Owens' point. All that he wanted was for *The Baptist Program* not to represent the official voice of one side of an issue and fail to give equal voice to another when Southern Baptists would divide almost equally on the issue![9] *The Southern Baptist Journal* began to be printed for the purpose of airing a total issue, not just one side. The issues of December, 1973 and January, 1974 prove the intent of the editor to be fair.[10] State papers seem also to have a tendency to be or become house organs rather than forums, except for letters to the editor.

Mr. Owens has a long record of denominational service to his credit. He led two churches to give liberal gifts for the erection of the James P. Boyce Centennial Library at Southern Seminary and was also a campaign leader and contributor to Gardner-Webb College. However his opposition to structural changes in the organization structure of the North Carolina Baptist State Convention, Gardner-Webb College's move to a four year institution and leadership in the baptism issue in North Carolina has led him to be anathema and is the "No. 1" example to all pastors of what happens when opposition is voiced to the party line.[11] Fear brings only tokenism in giving cooperatively and in working together. Increase calls for mutual appreciation.

The great need for increasing gifts to cooperative missions is for each person receiving income in part or in whole to know that in someone's eyes *he is* the Cooperative Program and that he should be incessantly on duty as a public relations officer for the entire program.

One pastor, who at the beginning of his ministry was rather critical of the Cooperative Program but in later times had a real experience with the Lord and had his mind changed about many things, including a willingness to volunteer for foreign missions, found that regardless of internal spiritual changes within himself that Convention personnel would not forget nor put behind them that which he had been. He cried out in answer to the questionnaire that Convention people ought to "put more emphasis on where a man is than on where he's been; on his present motivation and commitment than on past history."

Denominational officials must seek to take our diversity and lead us to unity by becoming slower to take offense and show love even when their agents to the churches may be unlovely.[12] How a pastor feels can well affect mission gifts. This study has verified this truth.

Overcome error with truth. Footnote 9 on page 76 was inserted not in any means to downgrade the education of the six pastors involved, but to show that they had not been exposed to the kind of research and writing contained in a commentary of the nature of the Broadman volume on Genesis. Many pastors err on the side of fundamentalism because they simply have not had the opportunity to have in-depth study of the Bible in exegetical studies. Not having had the opportunity to arrive at truth, through formal study, and accept it, thought beyond present belief is branded as "liberalism." It is far easier to oppose something than to be for something. It is easier to lead a pack shouting old shibboleths than it is to be led to divine truth and to lead the pack in pursuing it.

Truth seekers are lonely people and are seldom believed in their lifetimes. However, the truths which they discover need as much defense as the lies hurled against them. As I look back over my brief life span, I can see that much of the "liberal" thought of the 1930's has become the fundamental gospel of the 70's.[13] It is not that basic truth has changed but that world conditions have stretched minds to a capacity capable of learning and retaining ever growing truth.

But what about those early truth seekers who arrived before the majority of their generation? Their truth lives but many of them failed to be accepted in their time and generation. This must not happen to today's truth seekers. When they are criticized they must be defended on the basis of Baptist's No. 1 doctrine: *the autonomy and competence of each soul under God.* The insistence on conformity by all to certain beliefs in order to belong, violates the autonomy of the soul to answer to God only. Without firm adherence to this belief, autonomy would have no meaning anywhere else. Autonomous persons create autonomous Baptist churches, associations and conventions.

Men of truth today must return to knowing the true meaning of the words of Julia Ward Howe when she wrote:

In the beauty of the lilies Christ was born across the sea,
With a glory in his bosom that transfigures you and me;
As he died to make men holy, let us die to make men free,
While God is marching on.[14]

The cost of this freedom is more than withholding
mission gifts but is to be paid in allowing each person to be
responsible to God for all that he does and permit God to
sit in the judgment seat on his actions.

In light of this, the Associational Promotional
Committee (or its equivalent in other Associations) must:

1. Answer criticisms of cooperative missions which come
to its attention by seeking to discover the truth and make
it known. It can best be done by

2. Presenting positive testimony for cooperative
missions.

(1) On a one to one basis – confronting sources of
error with the truth.

(2) Use the monthly *Gaston Baptist Bulletin* to
present facets of cooperative work which lend
truth to promote them and disavow the
misinformation purveyed by so many.

(3) Promote subscription plans for the *Biblical
Recorder, Home Mission* and *The Commission* to
assure adequate opportunity for each Baptist to
know what is being done with the use of
cooperative mission funds.[15]

(4) Include tracts in bulk mailings which uphold our
cooperative endeavors and to mail out periodically
helpful materials related to our common tasks
which may be to inform, inspire or lead to action.

SUMMARY

A common complaint has been that the Association, State Convention and/or Southern Baptist Conventions do not provide us with adequate information on how the money is used. The truth is, the material sent is just not studied. One of the questions asked of pastors was, "What would you like to say to the State Convention?" Nine of the thirty-nine pastors replied, "You ought to let us know the salaries and allowances received by State General Board employees. Everybody knows ours!" This information has been a part of the State Convention's annual financial report for years and is found in that section of the Annual.

I had a special advance section in the Association's thirteen page annual calendar one year because the complaint was raised, "You don't tell us far enough ahead." By count, twenty-three pastors called in for information which had been on their desks for months and had planned conflicting arrangements long after data was in their hands to prevent conflicts.

Johnson and Cornell[16] say 48% of the laymen read printed materials coming to them thoroughly, and 49% skim the material. It seems that pastors fail to maintain this high ratio of reading and reviewing materials which come to them.

In seeking to answer criticisms of liberalism in our seminaries the author made a study of the amount of a given $100 gift from any church which eventually reached a seminary professor. It proved to be .0072 cents of each $100, or it took a $200 gift to permit 0.144 cents to reach the so-called liberal professor. On being provided this information one pastor said, "I want no part of it. A little leaven leaveneth the whole lump!"[17] He was reminded of

54

Matthew 7:1-2. This seems to be the only answer to such *picadillos*. *Attack Unknowing With Knowledge – Church Mission Organizations*. I prepared work papers which show how well the churches were organized to teach missions as it related to mission organization structure, use of weeks of prayer, mission study, and Baptist publications concerning missions being received in the homes. It was found that those best organized to teach missions did the best job in keeping up mission percentage gifts and raising money for missions. The fact is that of the twenty-six churches studied, the twenty-three that did the best job were fully organized to teach missions. All of this information is reflected in the 1974 Annual of the Association. Therefore, unknowing can best be eliminated by using existing church organizations for the purpose of letting the people know what is going on.

It is suggested that the Associational mission organizations increase their efforts to organize and train workers in the churches to provide a full program of missionary education as follows:

1. Membership, attendance, good programs, mission action.
2. Weeks of Prayer for all areas of mission endeavor
3. Annual Home and Foreign Mission studies – churchwide
4. Attendance at summer assemblies and/or camps

It is suggested that the church council and/or pastor emphasize missions as follows:

1. Missionary preaching and teaching
2. World Missions Weekends. See Appendix III for complete resume of this program.

3. World Mission Conferences — which ought to be held at five year intervals in all associations.

4. World Mission Month. See Appendix IV.

It is suggested that the Associational Executive Committee seek to overcome unknowing with knowledge in the following ways:

1. Mission emphasis associational meetings

2. Publicize cooperative work between cooperative missions and the Association

3. Mission emphasis annual calendar. See Appendix V.

That this kind of teaching program works can be observed in the fact that the author contacted his longtime personal friend, Dr. Carl Compton, Pastor, First Baptist Church, Myrtle Beach, S.C., and asked how he led the church to give thirty cents of each offering plate dollar to missions, and he replied:

(1) We have *informed our folk* regarding the *mission needs* of our world —

    A. By putting our state paper in our budget.

    B. By observing an annual Foreign Missions Day in December with a missionary family as our weekend guests and speakers.

    C. By having state leaders as pulpit leaders from time to time.

    D. By using students from our Baptist colleges in special programs occasionally.

    E. By making the Week of Prayer emphases Church-wide.) For several years our men have led the Wednesday night programs in these.)

    F. By preaching about world needs and

    G. By providing printed materials on the Cooperative Program.

(2) We have *encouraged* a *percentage gift* for

missions for a decade instead of a set amount in dollars and cents. As more is given, more goes outside the local church.

(3) We have *encouraged* a *step up* of one or two percent *each year* in mission gifts as the budget has been proposed. (At first it required some convincing of the folk, but now it is expected.)

(4) Our *goals* for the special missions offerings have been *set* at *15 percent above* what was given the previous year. (We have used "indicating devices" to mark out progress. Note enclosed clipping regarding 1973 Lottie Moon Offering.) These goals are adopted by the Church during Church Launch Week at the beginning of the year.

(5) Our *total stewardship* program has been *undergirded* by full monthly *reports to the people* of our giving and the use of their gifts. (When spending at home has seemed too great the folk have expressed concern that we are forgetting our major purpose.)

(6) Our *approach* at *Budget Time* has been:

    A. Our concern is for the *needs* of the whole *world*, and

    B. We believe *you want to share in* this, so

    C. Make a worthy gift to a worthy budget — and the response has been good.

Also, Douglas Aldrich, Pastor First Baptist Church, Gastonia, whose church is twelfth in total gifts to the Cooperative Program in North Carolina, although it is far from being the 12th largest chucrh in size, indicates the same type program is effective in that church. J.D. Williams, Pastor First Baptist Church, Mt. Holly, N.C., whose church consistently gives more per capita to the Cooperative Program than any other church in North Carolina, indicates that this is the program used that does the job there. The author also notes that the longevity of the pastors in these three churches is a significant factor (Compton, 25 years; Aldrich, 12 years; Williams, 22 years). *Counter Inequities with Fair Share — Stewardship Committee.* Since most of the pastors admitted to a knowledge of increased dollars not necessarily meaning increased mission support, it seems that this fact must be ever kept before church budget planning committees, as one participant in interview said, "Whether missions get more money or not often depends on who makes the motion." True, but it ought not be so.

The Associational Stewardship Committee must teach program budgeting[18] to the church finance committee and also lead them to long range planning. Adequate materials and helps to do so are readily available from the State and Southern Baptist Convention offices dealing with these matters. Plans are underway for such helps to be made available in 1975-76 to the churches. Plans are to suggest a 30/70% split of the offering plate dollar as fair share for missions sharing and local work, with 20% undesignated to Cooperative Program and 10% to be used for various designations to Associational Missions, state objects, and specials to Lottie Moon Christmas Offering for foreign missions and Annie Armstrong Easter Offering for home missions, and such others as the church chooses. One pastor felt it unfair to count only undesignated funds as Cooperative Program where 90% of all other gifts go to the same objects. This might need to be reconsidered by statisticians who account for the various funds. If the

Gaston succeeds in going 30/70%, North Carolina ought to go 40/60% and the Southern Baptist Convention 50/50% in the United States and foreign missions.

Our concept of A FAIR SHARE for the local church is as follows:

Church Use	.70
Cooperative Program	.20
Assoc. Missions	.02
Other Missions	.08
(Annie Armstrong,	
Lottie Moon, State	
Missions & Others	
	1.00

Each offering plate dollar so shared would provide adequately for *all* missions. We could then do something other than preach the gospel to ourselves.

Absorb Individualism Into Community (Koinonia). All of the Association working together.

One of the most essential things to be done in this Association is to build a fellowship based on trust, love, understanding of one another, and our common purpose which has been described earlier in the purposes of the Association.

William G. Dyer, in writing *The Sensitive Manipulator: The Change Agent Who Builds With Others*, indicates that it can be done only by caring for one another and having open communications with no fear of being ostracized. Differences are bound to arise when two or more people are working at a common task. Trust is the basic and cardinal principle on which all society hinges and can be built only when one person believes that the other person is basically honest and is seeking to do the best he knows. Another way of putting it is that we must so care for one another that we are willing to trust them as much as we want to be trusted by them, and have such an openness between us we will seek to make ourselves known even as we wish to know others.

Trust leads to love and love leads to understanding because "love covers a multitude of sins." This simply means the eyes of love do not look on a situation with the same eyes in which no love light glows. Caring for is the end result of love which has been bolstered by the openness and trust which are necessary for men to work together in common purpose.

Johnson and Cornell remark that the historic purpose of the church has always been "its reach beyond its own hallowed sanctuaries. And that is what its American members want, that the church concentrate on sowing seed in wider fields, on calling a wavering civilization to faith, on being about its mission."[18]

This must continue to be our purpose if we are to do mission in our setting in our time.

WHAT HAS BEEN DONE?

The reader will note from much of the material included in the appendices, a great deal of work was done in the 1972-73 and 1973-74 church years toward carrying out the strategies included in Chapter Three of this work.

Deepening of Fellowship

The fellowship of the pastors has improved immeasurably as a result of working together in groups completing their church charts and answering questionnaires, and just talking in general about Baptist missions, as the work was being done. It has been amazing to hear the pastors discussing facts about their church records which one would have thought they already knew. One pastor was shocked to find his church paid more for pastor remuneration five years ago than now. Most were shocked that mission gifts had decreased in percentage and many in dollars. Resolves were heard to overcome the condition and get back to a greater sharing of the gospel. One of the best things to come from the project was these discovering and sharing sessions. The men seem to have drawn closer together and have more personal contacts than heretofore, and have been more agreeable in committee meetings in overcoming common problems.[1]

Greater Awareness of Common Purpose

In the midst of this section the author had to undergo

surgery and subsequently suffered a stroke. How deep the fellowship has become can be well evidenced by the care and concern shown him by pastors and members of the churches in notes written, in cards, and expressed desires for the carrying out of all that we have begun together through the field experience and this written project. The pattern has been set and is well on the way to functioning even without the Superintendent's presence on the job. This was an unexpected testing of the value of the work.

Percentage Decline Slowed With Gifts To Missions 1973-74

Table V, page 19, will indicate that gifts have slowed the gradual slide to lower percentages and that in most instances percentage increase is underway.[2] Where it did not show favorably in 1972-73 and 1973-74, the pastors are now aware of the problem and are at work to do more for missions in 1974-75 than in the past.

Projected Increases in 1974-75

The questionnaire answered by the pastors called for percentage goals for 1974-75. According to their answers the Association will provide well over $1,000,000 for cooperative missions in the current year, with nearly $750,000 to Cooperative Program undesignated.[3] The Association had twenty churches in 1972[4] which made no gift to the Cooperative Program but of these, sixteen are on a subsistence level and four have the "liberal" bias. However, these four contribute more to cooperative missions designated than they contributed to the Cooperative Program before they "fell out" over liberal professors.

Prognosis

It is the Association's purpose to give assistance to those churches which just exist and seek to bring them in a little closer by this aid. Working by securing aid has already worked in three instances and leadership feels that progress will continue to be made until 100% participation is reached in cooperative missions. In the three instances referred to help was given one by securing a gift from State Missions for $2,000 and sending six "Associational" missionaries from one church to tithe, teach and give time toward guiding it back to strength. In eighteen months the church was back on its feet and the $2,000 gift returned three times over in gifts through the Cooperative Program. The six "missionaries" returned to their church blessed time and again in the months of sharing.

A second church heard of the work and requested assistance which was sent in the form of three workers for one year, who helped them write a constitution, call a pastor and secure pastoral salary supplement from the State Convention. The joys of this help were found in similar love for cooperative missions but most of all in the church's becoming alive to a sharing of the gospel which led that fifty-six member church to reach and baptize forty-four new converts in the first year of its return to full church status.

The third church was helped in securing lot aid from the State Board in order to rebuild its building. It went from nothing to $500 undesignated to Cooperative Program plus another $700 to other cooperative missions the very next year after help was given.

It is believed that similar helps given to the remaining eleven churches will end in increased and full participation on the part of all our churches in not more than two additional years.

One pastor replied to the question, "Why do you support the Cooperative Program?" with "It's the most reasonable and specific way to obey Christ's command."[5] Nothing else needs to be said; we need only to do it.

OTHER PROPOSED HELPS

Program Budgeting

I believe that the one single best help for mission giving will come when the churches come to Program Budgeting: a procedure through which funds are allocated to carry out the plans of the organizations, officers and committees of the church.

Practically every church follows the procedure in presentation of budget as did those churches I guided across twenty-two years. The amount for an item was shown in one column for the past year and the proposed new year in a column adjacent to it. Then a third column would show the increase or decrease for the new year. Needless to say, we spent many a "happy" hour getting budgets adopted as the figures were argued, compared and revised. The figures were generally compiled and budget proposed on the basis of expected cost increases by persons who had little or no knowledge of that which needed to be in the church program and was argued by people who knew even less.

Then one year we got smart and had the various officers, committee chairmen and organizational heads to plan their year and request money to carry out their plans. These figures went to the finance committee, which put all of it together for presentation to the church.

The first year of this procedure brought on some

complaints of "How much did we spend for this last year?" but a ready answer was, "It's no matter! This is what is needed to cover plans for this year." The budget passed with little or no emendations from the floor. Generally, the only item which brings discussion is staff salary increases and these are now based on cost of living index and when explained, most generally ends in little strife or factions.

If program budgeting could be followed with each section of the budget being set up on percentages of the total rather than by set amounts, each item in the budget could expect normal increases from year to year.

The problem of most churches is that increased dollars do not mean an increased percentage of total income going to missions. We can take pride in giving $1,000 to cooperative missions in a new budget if the dollar amount for the past year was less than $1,000, but if the total offering plate dollar increased 20% and mission gifts only 10% you can see an imbalance will take place just as it did in the Gaston Association as shown in this study.

Percentages should be set in program budgeting and adhered to in planning that a fair share can go to all the world. We believe that the share suggested (70% local, 30% missions) is realistic. It would provide from our Association alone, $1,200,000 annually undesignated to the Cooperative Program and $600,000 for other missions. This is twice the current rate of sharing for cooperative missions.

Through programs budgeting and maintaining a proper balance in percentages going to missions, salaries, organization expense, services, maintenance, new building and/or debt retirement everything in the local church program could be cared for with ever increasing dollars from a constant fair share going to all the world.

This type of budgeting also provides a standard by which to measure results in the various programs and plans. At the end of the year reports should be given on that which was accomplished by the expenditures and serve as a basis for the next year's plans and projections.

The Baptist Press and Opinion

I have shown previously (p.46) the utter impossibility of getting the message of missions to the people because of lack of readership of the Journals and State Papers.[1] I feel that this can be remedied by beginning that which I call *The Baptist Press and Opinion* for the lack of a better name. If this proposal to aid missions is carried out, it would make a decided change in our present publication arrangements of most of our Boards and State papers.

I hope that I have convinced my readers of a needed change, but am aware, "that in many areas most people want change, but that the democratic defense of minority interests too often inhibits general change."[2] But if our purpose is for "eliciting, combining, and directing the energies of the denomination for the propagation of the gospel...,"[3] we should give serious consideration to the idea which would help us to overcome our local and state selfishness in looking at a larger field of interest and service.

The problem of declining percentage in church gifts to missions also is to be found in North Carolina's percentage of gifts through the Cooperative Program sent on for Southern Baptist Convention purposes.

Some years ago North Carolina shared 40% of all Cooperative Program income with Southern Baptist Convention causes; however, in the last few years it has declined to 33.34%. The 40% figure is the amount which we suggest in our "Fair Share" proposal to be the shared figure on State level as

Church   70% – 30%   State
State   60% – 40%   Southern Baptist Convention
SBC   50% – 50%   Foreign Missions.

If North Carolina had given 40% in 1974, $636,140[4] more would have been available for Southern Baptist Convention purposes. So we see that as Gaston Association has declined in percentage giving, so the Baptists of North Carolina and World Missions suffer because of our "democratic defense of minority interests."

The way to overcome it is to be found in the founding of a weekly paper of *Baptistwide* interest which would pull us from localism to "lengthen our cords and strengthen our stakes."[5]

To me, it ought to be patterned after *The National Observer* (see Bibliography) in format and designed for general readership over the nation and world. It should contain current news and articles of national importance written from a Baptist perspective, and deal with all areas affecting our lives. In addition, it would contain on the spot analyses by our people in foreign lands when the items become of world interest such as hunger, aggression, change, in governments, etc. It could also contain many of the human interest and mission articles as carried in *The Commission, Home Mission,* or *World Mission Journal,* and find larger readership and impress more people to action.

I think, too, that much of the *Home Life* publication of the Sunday School Board could be better used in a weekly newspaper of this nature.

The editorial page could use the best of the wider

interest editorials of the state papers and the editors of them be considered contributing editors to the *Baptistwide* Journal or serve on the Journal's independent Board of Directors. However, it is my opinion that the Editors and Managers of the weekly be wholly and totally responsible to its Board and the Southern Baptist Convention as all other Boards and agencies are. They would hold their own opinions *consistent* and in keeping with the freedom enjoyed by other publications of national circulation.

It ought to be set up as a profit making enterprise employing Christian newspaper people to manage, direct, layout, edit and circulate. It ought to pay competitive salaries, sell advertising space for products or services not offensive to Christian conscience, set subscriptions rates and in general be free to operate in the open market to attract, inform, and inspire its readers to greater worldwide participation in meeting human need for and with the gospel of Jesus Christ.

I feel that profits ought to be used to make *The Baptist Press and Opinion* one of the nation's best publication houses and influential of public and denominational opinion. When that is done its profits should be given through the Cooperative Program as a state convention's gifts are given.

I will even let my own localism show by saying its publishing house ought to be located away from centers of present Southern Baptist influence but near enough for instant communication or contact by air travel, rail or highway. It should be where the facility for rapid circulation is available and in a proven stronghold of Baptist cooperation such as Gaston County, North Carolina.

I feel that should such a weekly be established that state

papers, board journals and/or publications may have to rethink their purpose and how best to share their present materials for the greater good and how to better use themselves as promotional pieces, debaters of the issues, and wider use for news not of a *Baptistwide* nature.

I am aware that this proposal, if seriously considered by Southern Baptists, would cause consternation in many camps, especially the Executive Committee whose responsibility under the service of General Public Relations is "To properly relate the Convention to its many publics. . . ."[6] This, to me, would be the purpose of *The Baptist Press and Opinion* and would be open to more than the Executive Committee's opinion since *The Baptist Program* is not.[7]

I feel that *The Baptist Press and Opinion* would have wider circulation than all state papers, *Commission, Home Mission* and other general publications of other Boards herein discussed combined, and would serve as a better disseminator of mission information to more people and bring us closer together as cooperating Baptists with a World View.

Funding the press could be worked out by the Executive Committee and Interagency Council with as much public participation as possible. At first it might be more feasible to contract the printing and come to own the necessary equipment later.

Annual Day

A third help in improving gifts to missions would be an Annual Day held on the rirst or second Sundays following the close of the Associational year. Which Sunday would depend on the church's need to have time to complete its annual letter to the Association. It would be a day as suggested in the section on program budgeting to determine how the money for the last year had been used, to project plans for the next calendar year,[6] and to adopt a new budget.

The day would be used more or less in the same fashion as the annual associational meeting with the church taking a hard look at what it is doing in every area of its work, witness and service to its community.

When the day was over, the church would have looked at the past year, adopted a new program budget and approved its uniform letter to the Association. In addition, there would have been worship in the morning, fellowship at the noon homecoming-style dinner, and a mission speaker for the afternoon.

Such a day would inform, inspire and lead all participating members to action in the total mission of the church in its setting.

I tried the idea the last two years of my last pastorate. The first one became little more than a Sunday off because I had not laid the proper groundwork for the day. However, the second met with moderate success after the church learned that it was not only review, planning, but also budget adoption day. We did the latter last to hold the people through the entire annual day program.

Fifth Sunday Mission Emphasis

The Committee of Fifteen's Report suggested that the Sunday School Board should consider returning to a former practice of including mission material in its curriculum. I would like to add testimony to this need.

As a child my pastors were very missionary minded and

preached often on this theme, but there were no mission training organizations for boys and men. My first remembered contacts with mission study were when, at age twelve, I began attending B.Y.P.U. and found that each fifth Sunday night the program was on missions, and under the direction of the Union's Treasurer. Being Treasurer, I often found myself having to give more than one part. The Union may not have learned but I did, and began a lifelong interest in this area of service.

Largely, all that I learned in this important area, until I began study for the ministry, was learned in this way. So the twig was bent, but what if it had not been?

I believe the fifth Sunday in every church should be devoted to the teaching of missions. Knowing that the Inter-Agency Council has assigned the task of teaching missions to the Woman's Missionary Union and Brotherhood, it might create some curriculum problems, but none which could not be answered by the Sunday School Board's asking these organizations to write the curriculum materials for these fifth Sunday programs, giving due credit and permitting them to use the space to also promote the organizations as needed. It seems to me that we're all in the same business and that handling missions for everyone in this fashion would be a better sell. General promotion for the Easter Offering for Home Missions, Fall Offering for State Missions, Christmas Offering for Foreign Missions, as well as the Cooperative Program and Associational Missions could be handled on one of the four Sundays available for this each year.

The church could also call in furloughing Foreign missionaries, nearby Home missionaries, or have the pastor preach a missionary sermon. This quarterly emphasis would create an awareness for every attending member of the church.

I did not use the fifth Sunday for this purpose in pastorates but feel the Baptistwide observance of the regularity of the fifth Sunday would improve on what I believe we began in the churches of North Carolina in 1952, that is the churchwide observance of Mission Study in the Winter and Spring.

I felt that men and boys did not attend because no one acted as if they should. With my teaching and inviting the men and boys, before long their attendance began to outstrip the women and girls, even when the guest teachers were the pastor's wife or other women. The entire evening program was given to mission study and proved its worth in increasing gifts to missions in the three churches which I served before being called to my present work.

I think the heads of our Southwide Boards and Agencies could design a suitable fifth Sunday curriculum which would prove a blast off for missions.

73

NOTES

Chapter One

[1] *Associational Administration*, "The Ridgecrest Statement," Home Mission Board, July 1974, Vol. 8, No. 7, p. 1. It is appended in full.

[2] Pope, *Millhands and Preachers*.

[3] Bennett, *The Fellowship of Kindred Minds*, p. 138.

Chapter Two

[1] Cope and Wellman, *The County of Gaston*, p. 3.

[2] Mayberry, *Mine Eyes Have Seen the Glory*. The oldest inscription is dated: Edward Boyd, July 28, 1728, p. 22.

[3] *Ibid*, p. 22.

[4] Cope and Wellman, p. 4.

[5] Most N.C. counties have one large city and several small ones. Table I is a summary in ten year spans of the population of Gaston County by towns and townships since 1910 with projections to 1990.

[6] Clay and Orr, *Metrolina Atlas*, p. 3.

[7] Remnants of the works can still be seen in a sealed off section beneath High Shoals Mill in High Shoals.

[8] Table II gives Gaston County employment from 1950 and is projected to 1990.

[9] Pope, *Millhands and Preachers*, p. 208.

[10] Cope and Wellman, p. 167ff. and Pope, p. 24, Footnote 5.

[11] *Population and Economy*, p. 69.

[12] Clay and Orr, p. 74, give the owner occupancy rate at 60-70%, with an average value of $13,000-$14,500. This stabilization is reflected in Table IV, Population Analysis.

[13] These were $2,885 and $9,507 respectively in 1970.

[14] Pope well points up this problem in Chapters 4-6 of his work.

[15] Hamilton, *The World's Great Religions*, p. 20.

[16] GBA, 1974, p. 96.

74

[17] *Ibid.*

[18] Purefoy, *History of the Sandy Creek Baptist Association*, p. 46.

[19] Mayberry, p. 22.

[20] Pope, *Millhands and Preachers*, p. 104.

[21] Pope, p. 105.

[22] Whitley, *Gaston County Baptist Church History*, contains individual articles on each church.

[23] *Gaston Baptist Association Annual*, 1919, p. 3. Hereafter the Annuals will be listed as: GBA, 1919.

[24] *Ibid*, p. 5.

[25] Data for the table is taken from the Annual of the years shown.

[26] GBA, 1919, p. 5.

[27] GBA, 1920, covers.

[28] GBA, 1933, p. 23.

[29] GBA, 1920, pp. 9-36.

[30] GBA, 1929, Tables I and II.

[31] Interviews with Walter Long and E.G. Powell.

[32] GBA, 1944, p. 13.

[33] Interview, T.L. Cashwell, Sr., August, 1973.

[34] Interview, E.G. Powell, March, 1973.

[35] *Ibid.*, Mr. Powell was a member of the Executive Committee at the time of the controversy.

[36] GBA, 1945, p. 14, and GBA, 1964, p. 11.

[37] Hoyle T. Allred, Field Work Experience, pp. 1-42, has a full history, word study and evaluation of these purposes.

[38] Murray G. Ross, *Community Organization*, p. 41.

[39] Given at a seminar, New Orleans Baptist Theological Seminary, February, 1972.

[40] GBA, 1919, p. 10.

[41] GBA, 1925, p. 22.

[42] GBA, 1923, p. 17.

[43] A member of a founding family of the Flint-Groves Baptist Church, placed her children in Flint-Groves School at its opening in 1927, and continues to support it vocally and by her presence

at every graduation since opening date. She finished the fifth grade. The last two grades were finished from seven to ten each night when Roy Sigmon, a Christian school master found her crying at having to quit school to go to work. He agreed to teach her and five others at these hours with parental permission and no extra pay.

[44]Pope, p. 271. In mentioning counter strategy, no mention is made of Christian service.

[45]Interviews of March, 1973. One person interviewed said that, Mr. Conn, President of the Loray strikers' union, used to come to her home and try to talk them into joining the strike. Her mother read in the Bible that people were to be "no strikers." The mother then told Mr. Conn, "We'll not join you." "All right," said Mr. Conn, the daughter remembers, "but if you don't join us, before it's over we'll be carrying you food." In the desperation of later days, Mr. Conn's family was fed and cared for by the community. Until this day the Conn family doesn't know where the help came from.

Chapter Three

[1]See Table VI, p. 24. For the purpose of this paper, the massive table has been condensed to years 1963, 1972, and a ten year summary. The years between will be referred to in the section, *Causal Factors Verified*, p. 28.

[2]Frank L. Perry, "A Suggested Procedure for the Funding of Agencies of the Southern Baptist Convention,", p. 139.

[3]Perry, p. 129.

[4]*Ibid*, p. 158.

[5]Table VIII, p. 30, summarizes the frequency of publication of motivating materials for the Cooperative Program in SBC publications referenced in these works.

[6]See page 29, material inserted and referenced as footnote 4.

[7]From the questionnaire.

[8]Johnson and Cornell, *Punctured Preconceptions*, p. 112.

[9]These six pastors unabashedly will tell you the *Commentary* was the issue. Four of the six attended Fruitland Bible Institute. The two others were high school graduates.

[10]Cooperative Program percent of total receipts dropped from 13.5% in 1970 to 12.3 in 1971, the first year of controversy. This is in terms of dollars $5,555 decline in 1971. How much can be attributed to the issue cannot be determined, but some by admission can be attributed to it.

[11]Elvin Jones in reply to the questionnaire.

[12]See page 27.

[13]See Table VII, page 27.

[14]Long Creek Memorial remained constant across the ten year period in percentage of total receipts going through the Cooperative Program.

[15]Perry, p. 158.

[16]See Table VI, p. 24.

[17]Chapter I of this work.

[18]Committee of Fifteen's Report to the Executive Committee of the Southern Baptist Convention, p. 6.

Chapter Four

[1]Most of the respondents made some reference to *The Associational Handbook*, which describes the organization of the Association and gives a job description for all officers, committees, and employed personnel. It was published by the Association in the late Fall 1972.

[2]The *Handbook*, p. 49.

[3]One of the great thrills of being the Director is to hear the comments of the pastors of the big churches and the small as the mission statistics are released each year and Gaston is No. 1! Each

is a member of the team and is shown that his part made it possible.

[4] See page 35.

[5] A colloquialism of the area which is applied to its fundamental beliefs.

[6] He wishes to remain anonymous.

[7] Elvin Jones.

[8] *Punctured Preconceptions,* p. 23ff.

[9] These facts come from numerous interviews from Mr. Owens on the matter.

[10] These issues carry articles on both sides of issues that are current among Southern Baptists, and it is the editors' promise that it always will adhere to this policy. However, in my opinion, subsequent issues indicate that the editor has a closed mind to positions other than his own.

[11] This is not a defense of what Mr. Owens does nor a defamation, but is to show his motivation and to show the reaction of Gaston pastors who have fellowship with him. Most of the time his position is reasonable to most pastors.

[12] The author is confident that a five year increase in Gaston Associational Missions has been occasioned not so much by an outstanding program but because the Superintendent seeks to practice the advice offered to others. People believe in people — not programs.

[13] Consider issues such as smoking, dancing, social ministries, race, recreation and immediately one sees what is meant by this statement.

[14] Julia Ward Howe, *Battle Hymn of the Republic.*

[15] More will be said in this area later in this work.

[16] *Punctured Preconceptions,* p. 23ff.

[17] Arson Dixon letter of April, 1973, written upon withdrawing from the Association because of the liberal issue.

[18] *Punctured Preconceptions,* p. 191.

Chapter Five

[1] One in particular was in writing and adopting guidelines for establishing new bus routes and missions. See Appendix VI.

[2] This can be discerned by studying individual church records of gifts to missions in the 1974 Annual.

[3] The one million was realized but only $601,372 went undesignated. However, $246,000 was designated to Cooperative Program objects.

[4] This was reduced to 11 in 1974.

[5] Paul Horne, Pastor, Cleveland Heights Baptist Church.

Chapter Six

[1] Also see Study Committee's report, pp. 12-13, Item 1 and p. 20 Item 6 for substantiation of my claims.

[2] The Report of the Study Committee of Fifteen, p. 6.

[3] Constitution of Southern Baptist Convention, "The Preamble."

[4] Computed from figures supplied by Dr. W. Perry Crouch. Statistics on page 117 of *Committee of Fifteen's* Report shows a general percentage decline of 4% from 1947 to 1971 from States to S.B.C.

[5] Isaiah 54:2c; The Study Committee's Report said (p. 13) that the decline in subscriptions to *The Commission*, "possibly could be corrected by making *The Commission* a magazine with more mass appeal." In my opinion this confirms the need I discovered which could be better met by *The Baptist Press and Opinion*. It would give balanced emphasis.

[6] In the Gaston Association, the associational year runs from October 1 through September 30, and most churches have or are moving to the calendar year for budget purposes. The weeks following Annual Day to the first of January could be used as needed for budget promotion.

BIBLIOGRAPHY

Books

Barnes, W.W. *The Southern Baptist Convention 1845-1953*. Nashville: Broadman, 1954.

Blalock, Hubert M. *An Introduction to Social Research*. Englewood Cliffs, N.J.: Prentice-Hall, 1970.

Clay, James W. and Douglas M. Orr, Jr. *Metrolina Atlas*. Chapel Hill: University of North Carolina Press, 1972.

Cope, Robert F. and Manly Made Wellman. *The County of Gaston*. Charlotte: Heritage Printers, 1961.

Dyer, William G. *The Sensitive Manipulator: The Change Agent Who Builds With Others*. Provo, Utah: Brigham Young University Press, 1972.

Garrett, Annette. *Interviewing Its Principles and Methods*. New York: Family Service Association of America, 1970.

Hamilton, Elsie. *The World's Great Religions*. Gastonia: *The Gastonia Gazette*, 1967.

Johns, Ray. *Executive Responsibility*. New York: Association Press, 1966.

Johnson, Douglas W. and George W. Cornell. *Punctured Preconceptions*. New York: Friendship Press, 1972.

Jud, Gerald J. and Others. *Ex-Pastors*. Philadelphia: Pilgrim Press, 1970.

Lindgren, Alvin J. *Foundations for Purposeful · Church Administration*. Nashville: Abingdon, 1965.

Lineberger, Jim and Vera. *A History of Hickory Grove Baptist Church*. Gastonia: The Hickory Grove Baptist Church, 1973.

Mayberry, Mrs. Roy M. *Mine Eyes Have Seen the Glory*. Gastonia: The Long Creek Memorial Baptist Church, 1972.

McGregor, Douglas. *Leadership and Motivation*. Boston: M.I.T. Press, 1966.

Paschall, George Washington, *History of North Carolina Baptist*, 2. Vol. Raleigh: General Board North Carolina Baptist State Convention, 1930.

Pope Liston. *Millhands and Preachers*. New Haven and London: Yale University Press, Paperback edition, 1971.

Purefoy, Elder George W. *History of the Sandy Creek Baptist Association*. New York: Sheldon and Co., 1859.

Schaller, Lyle E. *Hey, That's Our Church*. Nashville; Abingdon Press, 1975.

Schaller, Lyle E. *The Change Agent*. Nashville: Abingdon, 1972.

Schaller, Lyle E. *Parish Planning*. Nashville, Abingdon, 1971.

Scott, W. Richard. *Social Processes and Social Structures*. New York: Holt Rhinehart and Winston, Inc., 1970.

The Report of the Study Committee of Fifteen to the Executive Committee of the Southern Baptist Convention. Executive Committee of the Southern Baptist Convention. Nashville: December 21, 1973.

Torgersen, Paul and Irwin T. Weinstock. *Management an Integrative Approach*. Englewood Cliffs, N.J.: Prentice Hall, 1972.

Watson, E.C. *The Superintendent of Missions for an Association*. Atlanta: Home Mission Board, 1969.

Whitley, Dr. J.W. *Gaston County Baptist Church History*. Gastonia: Historical Commission of the Gaston Baptist Association, 1935.

Windley, Walter H., Jr. *Poor Folks at Home*. Gastonia: Gaston Community Action, Inc., 1966.

Reference Works

Cox, Norman W. *Encyclopedia of Southern Baptists*. Nashville: Broadman, 1958.

Cox, Norman W. *Cumulative Index to Articles in Sunday School Periodicals 1962-1964*. Nashville: Historical Commission, 1965.

Owens, John Joseph, *Procedure and Style Preference Guide.* Louisville: Southern Baptist Theological Seminary, Revised, 1971.

Southern Baptist Periodical Index. Single volumes dated 1965 through 1971. Nashville: Historical Commission.

Unpublished Materials

Allred, Hoyle T. *Field Work Experience.* The Southern Baptist Theological Seminary, Louisville, Kentucky, 1973.

Perry, Frank L., Jr. "A Suggested Procedure for the Funding of Agencies of the Southern Baptist Convention." The Southern Baptist Theological Seminary, Louisville, Kentucky, 1973, Ed D.

Hudgins, W. Douglas, "The Cooperative Program: Our Lifeline." The Executive Secretaries' Fellowship, Louisville, Kentucky, February 14-16, 1972, A Speech.

Periodicals

McCall, Duke (ed.). "Christian Stewardship," *The Review and Expositor.* Spring, 1973.

McClellan, Albert (ed.). *The Baptist Program.* Nashville: Executive Committee of the Southern Baptist Convention, July, 1967, October 1968, July 1969, April and November 1970, all issues of 1972 and 1973.

The National Observer. Dow Jones and Co. Inc. Silver Springs, MD. Published weekly.

Annuals

Gaston Baptist Association Annual. Single volumes dated 1919 through 1974. Gastonia: The Gaston Baptist Association.

North Carolina Baptist State Convention Annual. Single volumes dated 1963 through 1973. Raleigh: North Carolina Baptist State Convention.

Southern Baptist Convention Annual. Single volumes dated 1924, 1925, and 1963 through 1973. Nashville: Executive Committee of the Southern Baptist Convention.

APPENDICES

APPENDIX I

THE RIDGECREST STATEMENT

A report from the National Convocation on the Southern Baptist Association meeting at Ridgecrest Baptist Conference Center, May 6-10, 1974. 1. The future of Southern Baptist association is bright and promising. This positive forecast for the Baptist association was the consensus of the more than 1,200 participants in the National Convocation. Participants from across the nation included superintendents of missions, pastor, denomination workers and lay person. 2. Based on biblical principles, associations seek to relate churches to one another and the denomination. To fulfill their role, associations assist churches in many useful ways. Together and through the fellowship of the association, churches can have a broader and more meaningful ministry. 3. Major concerns help identify the role of the association: evangelism, missions, fellowship, doctrinal soundness, helping churches and providing a channel for training and information. The association is geographically the Baptist unit closest to the churches and exists to help the churches accomplish their tasks. The association is urged to recognize its setting and to assist the churches in their mission. The associations are encouraged to make a self study to determine their nature, needs, objectives, resources and opportunities. Such a study will help improve and strengthen programs of the association. Long-range planning for associational activities will give a sense of missions. Associations are encouraged to share their findings to strengthen state and Southern Baptist Convention agencies.

4. The association fosters a fellowship of encouragement, love, acceptance, and inspiration. Fellowship among Baptists is one of their strengths. The association strengthens and encourages fellowship among churches.

5. The association provides adequate organization to provide leadership in cooperative ventures. Many varied activities are sponsored and made possible through the association. Fulfilling meaningful and necessary roles has made the association a viable unit in Baptist life. Denominational leaders are urged to lend their support in encouraging the churches to give on a percentage basis to associational missions.

6. Essential to the association fulfilling its role is a well trained leader. It is suggested that the title "superintendent" be changed to "director" of associational missions. The strength of the director will directly affect the association. In a rapidly changing world, the need for continued education and training for associational leadership is urgent.

7. The seminaries are encouraged to increase curriculum courses and training events concerning the association, and to make available these courses in undergraduate as well as advanced degrees. The Division of Associational Services of the Home Mission Board and state conventions should encourage and provide assistance for training associational leadership. Associations are encouraged to support and help involve the director in a program of continuing education.

To equip and motivate church and associational leaders effectively, the director must stay abreast of current available materials, helps and emphases.
8. The Convocation reaffirms the historic pattern of cooperation among the associations, state conventions and Southern Baptist Convention agencies and institutions. The associations interpret, strengthen and promote support of cooperative Baptist work. The state conventions are primarily responsible for promoting the denominational program, receiving and remitting gifts for the cooperative ministries and enterprises supported by Baptist, and providing field services for various programs of work. The Southern Baptist Convention agencies initiate programs, reinforce and strengthen promotional and training events through providing literature, resource persons, field services, and national and/or regional conferences.
9. Associations can and should provide leadership for more effective communication. The use of public news and other mass media is encouraged. Today's world affords limitless means to influence people with a Christian witness.
10. Emphasis continues on a strong unity without compulsory uniformity among cooperating Baptist bodies. Participants in the Convocation leave Ridgecrest with optimism for the Baptist association and enthusiasm for its future.

APPENDIX II

A QUESTIONNAIRE FOR PASTORS
RELATIVE TO MISSION GIFTS

Part I

1. From your years of experience with Associational, State, and SBC missions, what would you like to say regarding mission gifts to each of the following?
    A. Your church finance committee.
    B. Your deacons.
    C. Your congregation.
    D. Your Gaston Baptist Association.
    E. Your North Carolina Baptist State Convention.
    F. Your Southern Baptist Convention.
2. Are there specific issues which you would like to hear discussed which relate to missions. If so, list them.
3. Are there specific reasons why you fail to support or do support the mission programs of your Association, State and SBC convention? Indicate "support," "Nort support" and which mission area in listing your reasons.
4. In your opinion, what are the strenghts of our Association?
5. What are its weaknesses?

(Use the other side of the paper or add sheets as needed in giving your answers to questions in this questionnaire.)

Part II – Specific Church Data

Name_____

Church Name _____

Size of Resident Membership _____

Location _____
      (open country, village, etc.)

Date your church was organized _____

Has your church added a new staff position in the last ten years?

Yes____ No____. If yes, what year? _____

Has your church built a new building during the last ten years?

Yes____ No____. If yes, what year? _____

The total budget of your current church in 1963 was
    $_____

Its total gifts to all missions in this budget were $_____

Its total gifts to Cooperative Program undesignated was
    $_____

What was your church budget for 1971-1972? $ _____

What were its total gifts to missions in 1971-1972? $_____

What amount was given undesignated to Cooperative Program? $_____

If there has been a decline or increase in these dollar amounts, to what do you attribute this change?

_____

Although you may have given more dollars to missions in 1972 than in 1963, is the percentage to missions of the total budget an increase or decrease?

Increase ____Decrease____.

    1963% to Missions   (Divide budget into mission
    1972% to Missions   gifts)

In your opinion, is this a fair percentage of your total budget to be going to take the Baptist witness to the world beyond your church doors?
Yes ____ No ____ . Give a reason for your answer, please.

Did your percentage of total budget given to the Cooperative Program increase or decrease from 1963 to 1972?
Increase ____ Decrease ____

    1963% to Cooperative Program   (Divide budget into
    1972% to Cooperative Program   Cooperative Gifts)

How do you account for this change in percentage of undesignated gifts to Cooperative Program?

_____

What is your church budget for the current year? $_____
What is the total amount for all missions? $_____
What is the amount undesignated to Cooperative Program?
$ _____
Are your planned gifts to all missions a percentage of the total budget increase over 1972?
Yes ____ No ____ .
Are your gifts through the Cooperative Program a percentage increase of total budget over 1972?
Yes ____ No ____ .
Are there reasons for your increase or decrease in these percentages of total budget? or, if you remained the same in these percentages, are there reasons for remaining the same?
Yes ____ No ____ .

please explain:

What are your percentage and dollars goals for the following in your current budget?

Association _____   _____

      (% of budget)   (dollars amt.)

Cooperative Program _____

             (% of budget)   (dollars amt.)

Part III — History and Planning

Check which of the following you have in your church:

GA's___RA's___Acteens___BYW___BW___

Baptist Men ___ Foreign Mission Study annually_____

Home Mission Study   Weeks of Prayer for

  annually _____   Associational Missions _____

Foreign Missions _____ Home Missions _____

State Missions _____ Lottie Moon Christmas offering _____

Annie Armstrong Easter Offering _____ Baptist

Bulletin Service _____   Biblical Recorder Club _____

Commission Club___Home Mission Club ___

Every family plan on either of the last three __Which? __ One or more mission volunteers__ How many __ What fields of service _____ Are your volunteers women__ men___?

        (number)

Plans

Will your church have participants in summer assemblies, 1974?

Yes _____ No_____

If yes, which assemblies? _____

Will these be for weeks designated as mission weeks?

Yes _____ No _____

Will you have youth at Mundo Vista ___ Caraway ___ South Mountain ___? (all yes or no)

Will you have participants in the Day Camp Workshop at your Baptist Building, March 26? Yes ___ No ___ Did you know about it? _____

Have you made plans to participate in the Associational. World Missions Conference, October, 1975?
Yes ___ No ___

Did you know one was scheduled for next year?
Yes ___ No ___

Do you want information on it? Yes ___ No ___
Please share name and date, if yes.

_____

Would you like to have such a speaker but have no contacts to obtain one?
Yes ___ No ___

If you have used any plan, program or method which has been successful in the promotion of missions and/or mission giving, would you please turn this page over and describe them on the back. Please turn over ___. We have none to share ___.

If you have personal objections to any board, institution or agency receiving funds through the Cooperative Program, which are they and why? _____

_____

How would you want your church members to handle their criticisms of you and your church program? _____

_____

Do you handle your criticisms of the mission programs in the same way? ___ If not, why not? _____

APPENDIX III

WORLD MISSION WEEKEND

An Exciting Experience of Foreign Mission Sharing

Purpose

To provide an in-depth experience in which members of the church may experience growth in awareness of foreign missions as they come to know and share with individual missionaries.

Planning

Church staff and council should discuss thoroughly the concept of a weekend Foreign Missions Penetration. Agreement on a format that will provide as many opportunities as possible for missionaries to have dialogue with various age groups of the church family is essential.

Personnel

Generally one to eight foreign missionaries from a variety of backgrounds and fields depending on the size of the church, churches, or association.

Program

Should involve several opportunities for the whole church groups, as well as other opportunities in which only a small segment of the church will participate. The following suggestions have proven to be useful in other churches.

    I. International Covered Dish Supper or Banquet on Friday night. Either the WMU or a group of women can be responsible for this occasion, providing international decorations. The Master of Ceremonies will have planned ahead of time, notifying each missionary that he will need to take from three to five minutes in which to introduce himself, state where he serves, and share one human interest story. A sharing time should follow with encouragement given to those who attend to ask questions about areas of concern and interest. While interest is still high the program is closed with a missionary devotional at the appointed time, approximately two hours from the beginning.

    II. Saturday offers time for various small groups to get together:

    1. A Brotherhood pancake breakfast. . .missonaries share personal experiences and answer questions.

    2. A WMU coffee at 10:00 am. . . . social time.

    3. A noon hamburger fry (autograph-time) for the Junior Department or mission organizations, after which the missionaries engage in an informal discussion time and fellowship.

    4. Saturday evening can be used for several home meetings with a missionary as guest in each.

    In a university setting, a Saturday night student banquet featuring international students as guests would give the missionary an opportunity for discussion with the college age group.

    III. The Sunday program plans are of paramount importance. Each missionary should direct the discussion for a Sunday School Department, realizing that this time of sharing may be the only contact he will have with some church members during the weekend. In larger churches, each missionary may need to visit two departments spending thirty minutes in each.

An option that can be exciting is for the pastor and one missionary to visit the elementary classes five minutes each for a get-acquainted and sharing time during the Sunday School hour.

The Sunday morning worship service should include a five-minute testimony by a member of the team plus a missionary message by a missionary in which he shared experiences from his own field and indicates some of the needs around the world.

Church Training Hour. . .a time for slides and discussion.

In some churches it may be well to have the entire team on the platform for a dialogue sermon at the evening worship service. For others, the more traditional service utilizing a different speaker than the one used Sunday morning will be preferable.

An additional option: Missionary reception following evening service.

Preparation

PREPARATION is the key to the success of the Foreign Missions Penetration. The consideration of such a program should be marked by earnest prayer as to the will of God in the matter. There must first be a consensus of opinion on the part of the church leadership that this type of program is desirable and exciting. Until a warm, open, sharing fellowship exists among the church leadership, a milieu for churchwide experience of this nature is difficult to bring about; therefore, spiritual preparation is imperative.

To be sure, the promotion of a Foreign Missions Weekend should be well planned and carried out. Don't take anything for granted — promote in every way possible.

Financial Arrangements

Responsibility for the travel, hospitality and honorarium (optional) for the missionary is accepted by the church, churches or association involved. The Foreign Mission Board will assist in locating the missionaries to be available for the Foreign Missions Penetration; however, the costs of promotion and personnel are the responsibility of the church.

For additional suggestions or answers to further questions you may write to:

Department of Promotion & Furlough Ministries
Foreign Mission Board
Box 6597
Richmond, Virginia 23230

Or to the regional offices:

Ralph West
Remington Building, Suite 204
100 17th Street, N.W.
Atlanta, Georgia 30309

Or to the Associational Office:

Hoyle Allred
Gaston Baptist Association
1607 Rankin Lake Road
Gastonia, N.C. 28052

APPENDIX IV

WORLD MISSION MONTH

The Cooperative Program was thought by many to be the answer to the financial support of all our agencies, institutions, and mission efforts of the Southern Baptist Convention. The Cooperative Program is the best way and will always remain the best way to support our cooperative efforts. But it has not been sufficient and it probably will never be adequate to take care of increasing needs. There are needs arising which cannot be met unless extra funds are made available. These funds must come by way of a special offering.

In North Carolina, we have many agencies which promote a special offering. For instance, our Baptist Hospital, Children's Homes, and Homes for the aging, rely on their income from the special offering as much as they do from the Cooperative Program. Our Foreign Missions, Home Missions, and State Missions are supported by both the Cooperative Program and Special offerings.

Meanwhile, back at the Association where the action is and where the offerings originate, the shoemaker's children are without shoes. The Association has been somewhat forgotten. No special offering is taken for its ministry. No allocations are made in the Cooperative Program for the Association. The Association receives contributions from its churches which usually remain the same year after year while the increase in mission giving is usually through the Cooperative Program and special offerings.

Why has the Association been overlooked? Perhaps because the Association has never been thought of as being a ministering agency. We think in terms of a man (Superintendent of Missions), an office, a mimeograph machine, and a question — "What does he do?"

What is the answer to the struggling Association? There is usually no trouble in financing the above concept, but a new concept is emerging. At least it is emerging in our Association and in many other Associations. The new concept requires more financial support. Where is this additional support? Some would suggest an easy answer — the Cooperative Program. Every Association would have its financial problems solved if ten percent of all Cooperative Program gifts were returned to the Association. But the "powers that be" would forbid such an arrangement. Therefore, our church has found what we consider to be an answer.

World Mission Month has been our answer, not only to associational needs, but it has given additional financial support to State Missions and Home Missions. How does it work? We designate December as World Missions Month. We do not take any special mission offering until December. Then, we take a World Missions Offering and divide the offering equally among the four mission areas — foreign, home, state, and association. We have a missionary to speak each Sunday in December with emphasis placed on the particular area in which the missionary serves. Each missionary informs the people of the mission work in his particular area and then relates his work to the total mission effort of Southern Baptists.

Why are we excited about this new approach? We like it for several reasons: because we have to promote a special mission offering only once during the year; we are able to give the same emphasis to each mission area; Associational Missions is not forgotten for it receives its share of the emphasis as well as its share of the offering; and because it makes December an even more exciting month.

If every church in our Association had followed this plan in 1970, our Association would have received an additional $10,620.75. This is over half of what we did receive from our 35 churches. Home Missions would have received $4,339.75 more than they received through their Annie Armstrong Offering and State Missions would have received $7,055.75 more than they received through their State Missions Offering. Our church, by using this plan, doubled the amount previously given through special offerings and we believe most churches could and would do the same.

We challenge you to try a World Mission Month and check the results for yourself. We believe you will like it, your people will like it, and the majority of our mission agencies will like it. Meanwhile, back at the Association, things are beginning to look a lot better.

(This program used by Raymond White while Pastor in Central Baptist Association. He is now Pastor of the Loray Baptist Church, Gaston Baptist Association.)

APPENDIX VI

SAMPLE CALENDAR

The two following calendar pages are representative of the twelve months in any given year, and show the mission and Cooperative Program emphases.

1975 ▣ MARCH

Gaston Baptist ASSOCIATION
FORWARD TOGETHER WITH CHRIST

1807 RANKIN LAKE ROAD, GASTONIA, N. C. 28052

Hoyle T. Allred, Superintendent of Missions
Mrs. Judy Cook, Office Secretary
Mrs. Dorothy Allred, Promotional Secretary
Yates W. Campbell, Director
Christian Social Ministries

GASTON
BAPTIST
BUILDING
Telephone **867-7257**

SUNDAY	MONDAY	TUESDAY	WEDNESDAY	THURSDAY	FRIDAY	SATURDAY
FEBRUARY S M T W T F S 1 2 3 4 5 6 7 8 9 10 11 12 13 14 15 16 17 18 19 20 21 22 23 24 25 26 27 28						**1** Regional Choir Festivals Pritchard Mem. Charlotte Children:10:00 Missions & Ministries Conf. March 1 (SEBTS)
2  HOME MISSION GRADED SERIES	**3** EXECUTIVE COMMITTEE BAPT. BLDG. 10 A.M.	**4** WEEK OF PRAYER for HOME MISSIONS	**5** Favorite verse:Ray England Pastor. Bingham Memorial "I love the Lord,because he hath heard my voice and my supplications. Because he hath inclined his ear unto me, therefore will I call upon him as long as I live." Psalm 116:1-2	**6** **Annie Armstrong Offering**	**7**	**8**
9 HOME MISSIONS DAY IN SUNDAY SCHOOL YOUTH WEEK Mar.9-16	**10** Metropolitan Missions Conf. Temple Church,Durham March 3-4	**11** WOMAN'S MISSIONARY UNION ANNUAL SESSION OVEN'S AUDITORIUM,CHARLOTTE Praising - Nashville,Tenn. Intro. new Hymnal M.10-13	**12** 8 Group Schools in Sunday School Work The Schools will be held March 10, 11 and 13 from 7:00-9:30 each evening. The books to be used are Working in Sunday School; Working With Pre-Schoolers; Working With Children; Working With Youth; and Working With Adults. Each book will be taught with each group of Churches and we encourage each church to participate with the group. Places and teachers will be announced in Gaston Baptist Bulletin.	**13**	**14**	**15** ASSOCIATIONAL BAPTIST YOUTH NIGHT FLINT-GROVES 7:00 p.m.
16	**17** ST.PATRICK'S DAY	**18**	**19**	**20**	**21**	**22**
		MINISTER'S CONFERENCE GARDNER-WEBB COLLEGE Vance Havner March 18-20 Featuring: Luther J. Thompson			N.C.Bapt.Youth Choir Festival Pritchard Memorial Church,Charlotte State Pioneers RA Congress Wake Forest University,W/S	Language Missions Conf. Camp CaRAway,Asheboro
23/**30** EASTER 	**24**/**31**	**25** PASTORS' CONF. BAPT. BLDG. 10 A.M.	**26**	**27** PASSOVER - THRU APR 3 Rural Church Conference Fruitland Conf.Center March 24-27	**28** GOOD FRIDAY	**29** APRIL S M T W T F S 1 2 3 4 5 6 7 8 9 10 11 12 13 14 15 16 17 18 19 20 21 22 23 24 25 26 27 28 29 30

1975 OCTOBER

Gaston Baptist ASSOCIATION — FORWARD TOGETHER WITH CHRIST

1807 RANKIN LAKE ROAD, GASTONIA, N. C. 28052

Hoyle T. Allred, Superintendent of Missions
Mrs. Judy Cook, Office Secretary
Mrs. Dorothy Allred, Promotional Secretary
Yates W. Campbell, Director, Christian Social Ministries

GASTON BAPTIST BUILDING
Telephone 867-7257

SUNDAY	MONDAY	TUESDAY	WEDNESDAY	THURSDAY	FRIDAY	SATURDAY
		Associational World Mission Conference Sept. 28 - October 3, 1975!	**1** COOPERATIVE PROGRAM PRAYER EMPHASIS EACH WEDNESDAY IN OCTOBER	**2**	**3**	**4** Baptist Women Retreat-Mundo-Vista / Pastor's & S.S.Directors Workshop Caraway- Oct.3-4 / Adult Sunday School Workers Workshop Caraway - Oct.3-4 / Younger Crusader RA Camp (Grades 1-3) Caraway - Oct.3-4
5	**6** FISHERMAN'S WORKSHOP	**7**	**8** PASTOR'S RETREAT PLACE TO BE DETERMINED	**9**	**10**	**11** Pastors & S.S. Directors Workshop Ridgecrest Oct.10-11 / DEACONS RETREAT, CARAWAY October 10-12
12 BIBLICAL RECORDER DAY	**13** COLUMBUS DAY EXECUTIVE COMMITTEE BAPT. BLDG. 10:00 / PROMOTIONAL COMMITTEE BAPT. BLDG. 11:00 A.M. / CANADIAN THANKSGIVING	**14** Praising Clinic 1st Church Forest City	**15** PRAY FOR	**16**	**17** Younger Crusader RA Camp Grades 1-3 - Caraway Oct. 11-18	**18** Favorite verse: Franklin Hartman, Pastor, New Life Church, "And God as able to make all grace abound toward you; that ye, always having all sufficiency in all things, may abound to every good work." II Cor. 9:8
19	**20** W.M.U. EXECUTIVE COUNCIL 12:15 / ASSOC. GENERAL BOARD 7:00 P.M.	**21**	**22**	**23** Gaston Baptist Association 57th Annual Session SANDY PLAINS, GASTONIA	**24** Gaston Baptist Association 57th Annual Session RANKIN LAKE, DALLAS	**25** SR. ADULT RETREAT-CARAWAY Oct. 23-25 / Festival of Arts Caraway, Oct.24-25 / Baptist Women Houseparty Ridgecrest - Oct.24-26
26 GIDEON SUNDAY	**27** VETERAN'S DAY PASTORS' CONF. BAPT.BLDG.10 A.M. / WMU MISSION ACTION CONFERENCE McAdenville	**28** S.S.Young Adult/Preschool Conference Charlotte - October 28	**29** MINISTERS' WIVES / THE WHOLE WORLD needs the COOPERATIVE PROGRAM	**30**	**31** HALLOWEEN	

SEPTEMBER
S M T W T F S
1 2 3 4 5 6
7 8 9 10 11 12 13
14 15 16 17 18 19 20
21 22 23 24 25 26 27
28 29 30

NOVEMBER
S M T W T F S
1
2 3 4 5 6 7 8
9 10 11 12 13 14 15
16 17 18 19 20 21 22
23 24 25 26 27 28 29
30

APPENDIX VI

GUIDELINES FOR ESTABLISHING NEW CHURCHES ID
AND MISSIONS OR NEW BUS ROUTES

The philosophy of Associational Missions is that God is concerned with the total vineyard as well as the individual vine (church). In view of this belief, we feel that God ·wants all people to be cultivated with salvation as its end; however, some are going untended while others are receiving multiple ministry. It is our belief, further, that guideline ought to be suggested to the member churches of the Gaston Baptist Association, to assure an adequate ministry to all people within our witness area.

Therefore, we suggest that in the development of mission points and bus routes that due consideration be given to assuring growing room for each church. In light of this, we suggest the following be taken into consideration when new work is to be established.

1. Is there an established church, mission or bus route affiliated with the Gaston Baptist Association in the area which we are considering for mission.

2. If there be, then those currently ministering, in the area being considered for ministry by a church, should be consulted and an agreement reached to prevent hindering a ministry already established and thereby rupturing the fellowship of the Association.

3. We suggest in establishing a new mission which is to become affiliated with the GBA that it not be done within one mile of an established work already in the Association in cities and towns; or 2 miles in the county areas unless the work already within the perimeter will agree.

4. No mission should be established in an area which is *adequately* being worked by a bus ministry.

5. No mission will be considered for affiliation with the GBA without sponsorship of an established GBA church. (Refer to Committee of Nine Report in the *Associational Handbook.*)

6. In the establishment of a bus ministry, that consideration be given first of all to bus ministries and/or missions, churches, etc., affiliated with the GBA which may already be established in the area under consideration. (Information to this effect is always available at the Associational Office.)

7. In setting up a bus route, we should not practice selective evangelism but are to evangelize people of all races and/or economic setting.

8. Sufficient teachers and leaders should be trained and Children's Church (or adequate worship experience) established before bus ministries are begun. Recall that we are to "build up" as well as to "reach out."

9. Be sure bus workers and Children's Church workers are thoroughly trained that what you begin might continue.

10. Under no circumstances should one entice a person already attending a church affiliated with the GBA, to leave that church and attend another.

11. In the use of promotional gimmicks, it should be kept in mind that we are not in a competitive business with one another — we are workers together with God. We are

in business for Christ and should do nothing to bring reproach to His name. In other words, be ethical in the use of gimmicks. Make Christ to be the most desired.

12. Remember in beginning a bus ministry it is to reach children in order to reach parents who will then become concerned for the child and total participation in the total church program.

13. Remember a bus ministry is mission. It is spending to reach the unconverted. Little remuneration will come at first. Bus ministry is a mission expense with no return expected but souls! If you don't have the funds to keep it going — DON'T DO IT!